Wheatley at 250

Wheatley at 250

BLACK WOMEN POETS

Re-imagine the Verse of

PHILLIS WHEATLEY PETERS

An Anthology

Edited by

Danielle Legros Georges
and Artress Bethany White

pangyrus

CAMBRIDGE

ISBN: 979-8-9862430-1-6
Library of Congress Control Number: 2023950059

Editors: Danielle Legros Georges, Artress Bethany White
Designer: Alex Camlin
Copyeditor: Rob Dobson

Black and African American Poetry
Women's Poetry
Black Poetics
Wheatley Studies

Published by Pangyrus Inc
2592 Massachusetts Ave #2
Cambridge, Massachusetts 02140
www.pangyrus.com

Printed in the United States

For general queries, contact Greg Harris, Editor at
editor@pangyrus.com

The editors wish to thank the Anonymous Donor
who helped us realize this book.

Contents

OF LIFE AFTER DEATH

ON RECOVERY OF HEALTH

TOWARD A NEW DAY

INTO THE FUTURE

OF CELEBRATIONS AND LIBERATIONS

Introduction

PHILLIS WHEATLEY PETERS has been called—and is—many things, including the young African girl enslaved by Boston's Wheatley family in 1761, and the acclaimed 18th-century transcontinental poet. In a magnificent 2006 essay, "The Difficult Miracle of Black Poetry in America," poet June Jordan names Wheatley "the first decidedly American poet on this continent, Black or white, male or female" by virtue of the keen attention Wheatley pays to the turbulent events of her time and the "revolutionaries who would forge America." Historian Henry Louis Gates, Jr., situates the poet squarely in the colonial and post-colonial debates that sought to confirm or dismiss Black intelligence. As a consequence of her distinction as a poet, Wheatley was thrust into a cosmopolitan sphere and found herself in conversation with such figures as George Washington and Benjamin Franklin (as well as posthumously with Thomas Jefferson whose 1785 *Notes on the State of Virginia* proffers scathing and undeserved criticism). Endorsers of Wheatley's 1773 book *Poems on Various Subjects, Religious and Moral* identified themselves as among "the most respectable characters in Boston" and included the governor and lieutenant governor of Massachusetts. They called her "a young Negro girl, who was but a few years since brought an uncultivated barbarian from Africa, and has ever since been, and now is, under the disadvantage of serving as a slave in a family in this Town." Of her poems, they remarked, "She has been examined by some of the best judges, and is thought qualified to write them." Less restrained, David Waldstreicher, a Wheatley biographer notes, "She became fluent and culturally literate and able to write poems in English so quickly that we shouldn't hesitate to call her a genius."

Recent scholarly attention to Wheatley's work includes Honorée Fanonne Jeffers's well researched 2020 collection of poems *The Age of Phillis*. Significantly, Jeffers advances the argument for referring to Wheatley by her married name. At the time of her death, she was still wedded to John Peters. This important historical detail liberates Wheatley Peters from perpetual historical adolescence; readers can now separate the celebrated but enslaved teenage poet from the free and married author. In her 2023 *Reading Pleasures: Everyday Black Living in Early America*, Tara A. Bynum, a scholar of literary histories, deepens our understanding of Wheatley's inner life by identifying her letters as a means by which Wheatley "delights in the pleasures of her living in spite of and because of the world-at-large."

Phillis Wheatley Peters called herself an Ethiop and African—and a poet. She dubbed herself friend to, among others, Obour Tanner, a fellow enslaved woman with whom she shared a lengthy epistolary friendship; Scipio Moorehead, a young African American painter; Samson Occom, a Mohegan Presbyterian evangelist; and Selina Hastings, Countess of Huntingdon, who was instrumental in the publication of *Poems on Various Subjects, Religious and Moral*. Wheatley saw her verse published in London and Boston, on two sides of the Atlantic Ocean. In addition to naming herself wife to John Peters, whom she married in 1778, she was mother of their children. Historian Cornelia H. Dayton, in the article "Lost Years Recovered: John Peters and Phillis Wheatley Peters in Middleton," offers a narrative that runs counter to the popular, unfavorable ones regarding what transpired between the Peterses. Among John Peters's chief efforts, she notes, was "to insulate his wife from physically taxing housewifery and to create space and time for her to inhabit a writer's life and to be a mother."

An acclaimed writer and political actor in her lifetime, Wheatley would not live to see herself as inspiration for an immense number of scholarly, literary, and creative texts. She would see neither the Boston plaque recognizing the site where she was purchased, nor her likeness in the form of a bronze statue on the city's Commonwealth Avenue mall, shaded by elm, sweet gum, and linden trees. She would not see the buildings and lecture halls named for her, hundreds of years after her unexpected death in 1784 while still in her early 30s. A second manuscript known to have been circulating at the time of her death has never been recovered, nor has the exact site of her grave at the Copp's Hill Burying Ground in Boston's North End been identified. While named for the ship Phillis that delivered her to the Americas and into the maw of the greed and attempted dehumanization that was the transatlantic slave trade, we will never know her West African name. Many, however, call her and claim her as *sister* and *ancestor*. Many name her the mother of African American literature, and a luminary of United States letters.

The idea for this anthology emerged in 2022 as we anticipated the following year as the 250th anniversary of the publication of *Poems on Various Subjects, Religious and Moral* on September 1, 1773, in London. As poets and editors, we understood the commemorative year as an ideal moment to revisit Wheatley—to get close to her, to approach her work from the shared standpoints and identities of women of color, Afro-descendants, and practitioners of one of humanity's oldest art forms. Moreover, and above all, we wanted the proposed encounters to privilege the poems themselves. We saw our project as an artistic experiment in the interpretation of Wheatley poems by *poets* and meant for 21st-century lay readers.

Toward this goal we invited the writers herein to each reinscribe, translate, or interpret a Wheatley poem—and to submit a brief compositional note to accompany her/their new poem. We envisioned each writer's contribution for the anthology consisting of three parts: an original Wheatley poem, a new poem, and a compositional note that would encapsulate their thoughts, considerations, questions, approaches, concerns, or wishes with regard to the creative process of rendering the "new" Wheatley poem. Our call made clear that this undertaking was not one of scholarship but of artmaking, of creating covers, if you will, in the way Nina Simone made "Feeling Good" by Anthony Newley and Leslie Bricusse inimitably her own, in the way Sinéad O'Connor re-did Prince's "Nothing Compares to You." We asked contributors to consider how their choices in language and form might reinvigorate Wheatley's themes and messages. As editors, we were keen to understand what could be demanded of us to keep appreciating and engaging Wheatley's work—and how to make her texts exciting to readers of various ages and experiences in this moment.

We were thrilled at how gracious the contributing poets were in their willingness to tackle the Wheatley poems we assigned them. What you will "hear" first is the writer's voice, followed by the new poem, and finally the Wheatley source text. In general, we chose Wheatley's shorter poems so as not to over-exercise the goodwill of our interlocutors, all practicing artists with busy lives. (We hope a future anthology might take up the long and other poems not featured in this book). We also attempted to align what we understood to be natural affinities or connections. Sharan Strange, for example, was asked to consider Wheatley's "To the University of Cambridge, in New England," because Strange herself had attended that august university in Cambridge. We asked the polymath musician and poet Janice Lowe to take Wheatley's "An Hymn to the Evening." This approach also left us delighted to have Jamaican poet Pamela Mordecai's recasting of Wheatley's "A Hymn to the Morning" in Patwa. A number of Wheatley's many elegies were distributed to poets we knew would approach them with supreme sensitivity. Gabrielle Civil, whose recent work mines the idea of memory, took up Wheatley's "On Recollection," and Rosamond King suggested to us "Phillis's Reply to the Answer" as one of the poems to be interpreted and "the only poem in which Wheatley mentions The Gambia, likely her place of birth, by name." King herself is a daughter of the Gambia.

Phillis Wheatley's international dimensions—biographical, educational, and linguistic—did not leave our minds as we worked on this project. The poets represented in the anthology are situated primarily in the United States, but also more broadly in an African diaspora containing landing points and connections to Jamaica, Haïti, Canada, and France—in addition to the continental nations of the Gambia, Ethiopia, Zimbabwe, and Sierra Leone.

The anthology is organized thematically, in the following categories that seemed to emerge organically as we reviewed the work: *Of Antecedents and Legacies; On Childhood; Of Life After Death; On Recovery of Health; Toward a New Day; Into the Future;* and *Of Celebrations and Liberations.* Some of the sections are longer than others for reasons that will be obvious, and we recognize that other groupings could have occurred. Within these areas fall poems and commentary compelling in their visions and styles, with approaches as singular and wide-ranging as the interpreters themselves.

We are grateful to the poets who accepted our invitation to make art in response to the verse of Phillis Wheatley Peters—and whose work constitutes this book. We are also grateful to Wheatley scholars in general, several of whom are referenced in this essay, and for *The Collected Works of Phillis Wheatley* edited by John Shields (the Schomburg Library of Nineteenth Century Black Women Writers, Oxford University Press), the source of the Wheatley poems that appear in this anthology (some appearing with minor variations). Our enormous thanks go to the editors of *Pangyrus*—Cheryl Clark Vermeulen, Amanda Lewis, Greg Harris, and Cynthia Bargar— who responded to our initial query about this anthology with an immediate and enthusiastic *Yes!* This book exists because of that yes.

What do we hope for with this project? We hope for a deepened engagement with Wheatley's poems; a willingness to struggle positively with Wheatley; an inclination to consider her as we consider ourselves: living and writing in a complex world that contains wars, enslavement, oppressions, the need to make a living, the being singular and representative simultaneously, and also joy. Ultimately, we hope this project will help make Wheatley's poems (in addition to her extraordinary biography and place in U.S. and international letters) better known and more accessible.

—*Danielle Legros Georges* and *Artress Bethany White*

Of Antecedents
and Legacies

Tracy K. Smith

I Trust that her Voice Had Roots in the Voices of Others

Survivor, herald, foremother, Phillis Wheatley Peters birthed a nation of poets. Though she was stolen from her own home and kin, I trust that her voice had roots in the voices of others. In this poem, I imagine her restored to the mothers, grandmothers, aunts, and neighbors at whose feet and in whose kitchens and on whose porches she ought to have sat. The virtue I'm listening for is the virtue those generations of women would have known and kept, and the gentle way they'd have taught it to a child in their midst.

ON VIRTUE

You are like the old ladies
my mother took me to visit
whose brown hands kept nimble
at small things. Shelling peas
on a porch or in a shady kitchen.
Stitching the hem of the world's
dress, which came loose every
so often. I thought you were the gate
through which I'd pass into bliss.

Ma'am—Sister—Aunt—Saint—
What I've learned, through ache
and shame, is a crumb
of what you stayed knowing:
Joy is a dark jar on a high shelf.
A spoonful can last a lifetime.
Widow—Keeper—Mender of Light—
To what new names do you now answer?
What the bowl sighs to the whisk.
How thumb greets husk. What
Night whispers into the nape of dusk.

On Virtue

O Thou bright jewel in my aim I strive
To comprehend thee. Thine own words declare
Wisdom is higher than a fool can reach.
I cease to wonder, and no more attempt
Thine height t'explore, or fathom thy profound.
But, O my soul, sink not into despair,
Virtue is near thee, and with gentle hand
Would now embrace thee, hovers o'er thine head.
Fain would the heav'n-born soul with her converse,
Then seek, then court her for her promis'd bliss.

Auspicious queen, thine heavn'ly pinions spread,
And lead celestial *Chastity* along;
Lo! now her sacred retinue descends,
Array'd in glory from the orbs above.
Attend me, *Virtue*, thro' my youthful years!
O leave me not to the false joys of time!
But guide my steps to endless life and bliss.
Greatness, or *Goodness*, say what I shall call thee,
To give me an higher appellation still,
Teach me a better strain, a nobler lay,
O thou, enthron'd with Cherubs in the realms of day!

Gabrielle Civil

Was I Wearing a Plaid Uniform Skirt the First Time I Read Phillis Wheatley Peters?

Was I wearing a plaid uniform skirt the first time I read Phillis Wheatley Peters? Probably. In high school, along with Langston Hughes, she would have been one of the few Black poets we read. It would have been only her most famous poem: "On Being Brought from Africa to America"—a true bait and switch. You think she's going to give you juicy details about her capture from The Gambia and her plummet into colonial slavery. Instead, she flexes her learning and uplifts herself via Christianity.

Wheatley's poem "On Recollection" offers a similar sleight of hand. Rather than recollecting her own intense past, she praises recollection itself. Calling on the Greek muse Mneme, Wheatley highlights memory as a creative force, a source of imagination ("her pomp of images display'd, / To the high-raptur'd poet gives her aid, / Through the unbounded regions of the mind"). Memory comes to embody art and expand awareness; it comforts the good and haunts the bad.

For those with sinful pasts, memory can be a terrible cross to bear ("Days, years mispent, O what a hell of woe! / ... the worst tortures that our souls can know"). On some level, Wheatley's speaker, in good Christian fashion, is yearning for a future to look back on past good deeds ("Be thine employ to guide my future days"). She craves positive memory as a peaceful shelter. She wants to skip ahead to the good part.

This gesture of flash forward inspired my remix poem "Of Recollection." As a Black feminist performance artist and poet, I am obsessed with Black feminist remembering, legacies, and experiential echoes (what I call *the déjà vu*). Wheatley's recollections profoundly informed (and troubled) future African American literary tradition. To this end, I decided to recollect, literally echo and mine, key lines from her poem along with lines from other African American poets navigating memory.

In order, the quotations in my poem come from "Nightmare Begins Responsibility" by Michael S. Harper; "cross-section of the schooner phillis" by drea brown; "Dope" by Amiri Baraka; "Nikki-Rosa" by Nikki Giovanni; and "good times" by Lucille Clifton. Harper recalls his newborn son's death; brown re-remembers/imagines Wheatley's arrival; Baraka takes on Christianity in Black historical memory; Giovanni and Clifton share family reminiscences. These voices together recollect my own constellation of poetic inspirations. They also showcase the rich creative future Wheatley projects and engenders.

Other phrases here also resonate for me. Wheatley's first two words are such an incredible speech act, I had to keep them. I italicized my own "vent'rous *Afric*" line to highlight awe and old-fashioned ideas of otherness. Her "long-forgotten calls" evoke my translated opening of Jacqueline Beaugé-Rosier's *A vol d'ombre* (*At Shadow Flight*); "we wake" echoes Sharon Bridgforth's amazing "bull jean/ we wake." I also gladly trade Maro for Mahalia Jackson and Aretha Franklin. With this remix poem I weave my remembering of the larger tradition. With reverence and gratitude, I wallow in Wheatley's recollections and celebrate my own.

MNEME begin.
I want to re-remember
vent'rous Afric in her great design
"hymns of *night-train,* train done gone"
    the long-forgotten calls
     nocturnal vision
    more like dreaming really
"bodybodybodybodybodybody"
   no not that part / I want bright
    celestial light diffusing
ev'ry tribe beneath the rolling sun
    tell it like it is
Sweeter than Mahalia's moans
Sweeter than Aretha's strains
    belt it out
"OOOO WOW! OOOOWOW!
it must be the devil
it must be the devil"
can't run from your past
went by in a flash / still lives in your flesh
    to be asham'd and mourn
"they never talk about how happy you were"
    more power to you
    pay the piper / change the scene
"good times / good times
   . . . think about the / good times"
    we wake and can't quite forget
    ev'ry holy, ev'ry upright heart
gets to regret and be/get the good

MNEME begin. Inspire, ye sacred nine,
Your vent'rous *Afric* in her great design.
Mneme, immortal pow'r, I trace thy spring:
Assist my strains, while I thy glories sing:
The acts of long departed years, by thee
Recover'd, in due order rang'd we see:
Thy pow'r the long-forgotten calls from night,
That sweetly plays before the *fancy's* sight.

    Mneme in our nocturnal visions pours
The ample treasure of her secret stores;
Swift from above the wings her silent flight
Through *Phœbe's* realms, fair regent of the night;
And, in her pomp of images display'd,
To the high-raptur'd poet gives her aid,
Through the unbounded regions of the mind,
Diffusing light celestial and refin'd.
The heav'nly *phantom* paints the actions done
By ev'ry tribe beneath the rolling sun.

    Mneme, enthron'd within the human breast,
Has vice condemn'd, and ev'ry virtue blest.
How sweet the sound when we her plaudit hear?
Sweeter than music to the ravish'd ear,
Sweeter than *Maro's* entertaining strains
Resounding through the groves, and hills, and plains.
But how is *Mneme* dreaded by the race,
Who scorn her warnings, and despise her grace?
By her unveil'd each horrid crime appears,
Her awful hand a cup of wormwood bears.
Days, years mispent, O what a hell of woe!
Hers the worst tortures that our souls can know.

Now eighteen years their destin'd course have run,
In fast succession round the central sun.
How did the follies of that period pass
Unnotic'd, but behold them writ in brass!
In Recollection see them fresh return,
And sure 'tis mine to be asham'd, and mourn.

O *Virtue*, smiling in immortal green,
Do thou exert thy pow'r, and change the scene;
Be thine employ to guide my future days,
And mine to pay the tribute of my praise.

Of *Recollection* such the pow'r enthron'd
In ev'ry breast, and thus her pow'r is own'd.
The wretch, who dar'd the vengeance of the skies,
At last awakes in horror and surprize,
By her alarm'd, he sees impending fate,
He howls in anguish, and repents too late.
But O! what peace, what joys are hers t'impart
To ev'ry holy, ev'ry upright heart
Thrice blest the man, who, in her sacred shrine,
Feels himself shelter'd from the wrath divine!

Of Childhood

Danielle Legros Georges
An Act of Literary Marronage

Beginning with its titular reference to geographies, Phillis Wheatley Peters's "On Being Brought from Africa to America" immediately signaled for me a doubleness to be explored. Repetitions—and rhymes, which exist in the original—seemed important in rendering the new text, as did ricochets and off-rhymes.

Wheatley Peters appears to address two audiences simultaneously: those who belonged, like her, to the community of enslaved persons, the African, the Negro black as *Cain*—and the implied user of the slur, the Christian, who is also the enslaver in the Americas. Employing two ontological systems—one in which her savior is greater than the god who allows her enslavement, and the other an adopted and expected Christianity—Wheatley engages in an act of literary *marronage*. She affirms and admonishes using the very terms of her captors, ultimately collapsing the externally imposed binary established to determine who is worthy of humanity and of heaven.

Because Wheatley credits mercy as a teacher, Mercy became a key for me, and an element to personify. I wanted to envision the girl-child who would become Phillis Wheatley Peters protected by a fierce and compassionate feminine force, perhaps one invoked by her first mother. I wanted to conjure up a surrogate mother who could bear and share knowledge that would keep the child alive and whole.

Humanity and heaven are posited as ultimate goals by Wheatley, who argues for their access and attainment by all Christians. What would happen, I thought (and in the serenely rebellious spirit of Wheatley), if I evoked an image of an afterlife not inconsistent with what may have been Wheatley's first spiritual beliefs. She is known to have relayed an early memory of her mother carrying out a ritual of pouring water before the rising sun. Why not call forth a Paradise containing the brilliance and nurturing warmth of that sun?

ON BEING BROUGHT FROM AFRICA TO AMERICA,
a reinscription

It was Mercy indeed
    Who carried me
        From what was deemed
            My *Pagan* land.

Mercy, you showed
    My soul to me, taught
        Me to understand that *God* exists
            —That something *Greater* exists too.

(Now, Mercy—Who knew

            (What) you (and I) knew?)

Some say & see the Dark
    As dead, as colored by
        A naught & dread. I say, I name
            Us fully: Cain: Daughters exiled,

Sons of rain. In us the flood,
    The moon & tides, horizons.
        uncut shores & lines, and more: the rays
            and versed libations to the waiting Sun.

'TWAS mercy brought me from my *Pagan* land,
Taught my benighted soul to understand
That there's a God, that there's a *Saviour* too:
Once I redemption neither sought nor knew,
Some view our sable race with scornful eye,
"Their colour is a diabolic die."
Remember, *Christians*, *Negroes*, black as *Cain*,
May be refin'd, and join th' angelic train.

Florence Ladd

I Marvel at her Knowledge and Deft Insertion of the Gods

Phillis Wheatley Peters's poem "On Messrs. Hussey and Coffin," was published in 1767. She was 14 years old. Her ode to those two men and their misadventure off Cape Cod is evidence of a prodigy. Moreover, her extraordinary command of English and capacity for empathy are unmistakable. No doubt the memory of her Atlantic crossing resonated with their plight.

I selected the poem for reinscription to allow me a sentimental return to Boston and Cape Cod, albeit vicarious. First, I had to renew acquaintance with the classics. Wheatley's familiarity with classical literature, referencing *Boreas* and *Eolus*, blew me away! I was reminded of my enthusiasm for the classics as a high school student. I marvel at her knowledge and admire her deft insertion of the gods in this poem.

An excursion into the meteorology of Boston's coastal waters for suitable vocabulary occupied me for several hours. The poem revived my memory of sailing into Boston Harbor, where a sudden storm's waves spanked the sails of my stepson's dinghy. I thought of *Moby Dick*, with Melville's incomparable terminology for oceanic weather. I then realized the poem is not about winds at sea; rather, it is about the experience of Hussey and Coffin.

Wheatley's many questions about their experience had me shift my focus from the water to the men. I copied her style of questions and appropriated some of her lexicon. Her rhyme scheme renewed my interest in rhyming. That my poem became a modified sonnet seems appropriate for the content, an 18th-century episode at sea.

On a shelf in my home library, I found *Life and Works of Phillis Wheatley* by G. Herbert Renfro, first published in 1916, reprinted 1969-70, and again reprinted in 1993, by the Ayer Company Publishers in Salem, New Hampshire. The book was acquired several years ago by my son-the-poet, Michael Ladd. In Renfro's introduction to the collection of her poems and correspondence, he wrote: "In the days when women were not encouraged to pursue the richer fields of science and literature, when only the wealthy and refined invaded the storehouses of ancient classics, a Negro girl became an honored precedent for an ungrateful nation." Many of her poems in this volume have an elegiac tone that influenced my reinscription.

I am grateful for the works of brilliant Phillis Wheatley and the occasion to honor her in this reinscription project.

ON MESSRS. HUSSEY AND COFFIN,
a reinscription

Hearing of your brush with death at sea,
young Phillis rushed to pen her wonderment:
how you endured tormenting winds,
pelagic waters buffeting your ketch.
Did you read the script in obsidian clouds?
Trembling, did you curse mythic wind deities?
Or pray to the *Great Supreme* that you,
Hussey and Coffin, spared briny graves,
be guided over the waves to Boston Harbor,
where hopeful and heartfelt relief awaited?
Did you thank *Heaven,* promising never again
would you repeat risking your lives at sea?

DID Fear and Danger so perplex your Mind,
As made you fearful of the Whistling Wind?
Was it not Boreas knit his angry Brow
Against you? or did Consideration bow?
To lend you Aid, did not his Winds combine?
To stop your passage with a churlish Line,
Did haughty Eolus with Contempt look down
With Aspect windy, and a study'd Frown?
Regard them not;—the Great Supreme, the Wise,
Intends for something hidden from our Eyes.
Suppose the groundless Gulph had snatch'd away
Hussey and Coffin to the raging Sea;
Where wou'd they go? where wou'd be their Abode?
With the supreme and independent God,
Or made their Beds down in the Shades below,
Where neither Pleasure nor Content can flow.
To Heaven their Souls with eager Raptures soar,
Enjoy the Bliss of him they wou'd adore.
Had the soft gliding Streams of Grace been near,
Some favourite Hope their fainting hearts to cheer,
Doubtless the Fear of Danger far had fled:
No more repeated Victory crown their Heads.

Janice A. Lowe

A Praise Party, a Celebration of Divine Creation, an Ode to All Things Sunset

My remix of Phillis Wheatley Peters's "An Hymn to the Evening" interacts with her delight and wonder in the bombast and nuance of the sun's red orange light and color parade through New England skies, and its eventual nightly, dramatic descent into Boston Harbor. In "Evening (the) Hymn," I imagine early evening visions and sounds a tender-aged Phillis may have experienced in the Senegambia of her earliest years, when she was a free child living with her birth family:

> *Equator-close, Africa's latest sunset, Home, sky's mango-hued stages,*
> *waves, fishermen, pelicans, Atlantic Ocean, Senegal River, Lake*
> *Retba's pink water, coastline Senegambia shoreline Boston, Maritime,*
> *maritime, free child in the world, before being sold into slavery.*

I wonder if Wheatley, in those few years after her forced removal from home remembered hearing *sabar* rhythms. (Sabar—a happening, a dance, drumming.) Does wordsmith Phillis use words as shiny bits of percussion in bigging up sunset's fascinating promenade? Spurred by Wheatley's love of using words as paint, I color in and around her bon mots. In my interplay, words and their insides play as objects, as musical instruments, utterances, singing, tint, and texture—syllables and lines that can be read or performed as counterpoint to the original.

Including the words "wood," "paper," "hemp," "ink," and "iron," I weave in letters representing textures and materials of a colonial-era military drum from Massachusetts, now housed at The Museum of the American Revolution. Did Phillis hear such drums while living the irony and hope of witnessing patriots' freedom-from-the-British aspirations, with little attention to abolitionism, to liberation of enslaved Black people? A third line of syllables drawn from my interaction calls, impressionistically, on *sabar* rhythms—bass sound, center drum, rim—sounding somehow on the page, and interspersed between the circadian rhythm of sunset words. If Wheatley heard that

Revolutionary War–era percussion, did those sounds jog her memory of the dynamic hands and sticks of *sabar*'s seven different drums? In her poem, I experience a word party, applause, and reverence for nature as only a writer can conjure.

My writing attempts to dance with/comfort the two Phillises, one pre-enslavement, and one after her enslavement: the Phillis who may have seen the sunset at Long Wharf near where her captured relatives landed and were sold, and the Phillis who may not have seen similar scenes, until she was caught up in the reality of that terrible economy.

In imbuing her word painting of the sunset with music, movement, symbolism, and cosmic wonder, Wheatley practices a self-conscious liberation of the mind and spirit that goes far beyond her nominal eventual freedom in colonial New England, and educates her readers about their shared humanity, starting with the acknowledgement of nature's precious everyday beauty and its enduring power to amaze.

.

EVENING (THE) HYMN
to sabar drumming: an impression/a celebration

abaNdon ink soon

On on on on

sky thuNders iroN

Nd nd nd nd

paper graNdeur peals

Nd nd nd nd

es sence flor et let tering

Ng ng ng ng

riv u let druM Ming

Um um um um

windy Fife reFrain

Re re re re

bird Warbling churCH

Ch ch ch ch

sabar song left of No rth

Th th th th

o range glo rious

Us us us us

hemp h u m

Mm mm mm mm

m**ing**　e　ther

Er er er er

God's at

mos

phere

Here here here here

shadow of cap　tu

red epiderm

is

S s s

ru by eve **n** ing soul s

N n n n

re **fresh** work

Sh sh sh sh

promise st**ee**led

Led led led led

stolen rep**O**se

O o o o

trunks tapped

Nk nk nk nk

Ta**pp**ed

SOON as the sun forsook the eastern main
The pealing thunder shook the heav'nly plain;
Majestic grandeur! From the zephyr's wing,
Exhales the incense of the blooming spring.
Soft purl the streams, the birds renew their notes,
And through the air their mingled music floats.

Through all the heav'ns what beauteous dies are spread!
But the west glories in the deepest red:
So may our breasts with ev'ry virtue glow,
The living temples of our God below!

Fill'd with the praise of him who gives the light,
And draws the sable curtains of the night,
Let placid slumbers sooth each weary mind,
At morn to wake more heav'nly, more refin'd;
So shall the labours of the day begin
More pure, more guarded from the snares of sin.

Night's leaden sceptre seals my drowsy eyes,
Then cease, my song, till fair *Aurora* rise.

Of Life
After Death

Kiki Petrosino

If Phillis Wheatley Peters's Poem is the Majestic, Green-Leafed Canopy, My Piece Suggests its Understory

In reinscribing "To a Clergyman on the Death of His Lady," I aimed to create a companion for the original. If Phillis Wheatley Peters's poem is the majestic, green-leafed canopy, my piece suggests its understory, that system of roots and soft-stemmed twigs composing the forest floor.

Wheatley's elegies brim with longing, not only to assuage the grief of their titular subjects (here the Reverend Thomas Pitkin, his late wife Temperance Clapp, and their children); they also wish to dwell in Paradise. I read these poems in landscape mode. They speak of home-going, evoking topographies personal and celestial, remembered and dreamed. What kind of heaven does Wheatley imagine at the moment of composition? How does her vision commingle New England and West Africa? I want to go there.

Wheatley's heaven resonates across symbolic registers. It's a place of "perfect bliss," where the soul attains wisdom inaccessible in life. It's also the ancestral "throne" and site of jubilee, where families reunite after death. "Amid the seats of heav'n a place is free," Wheatley counsels Pitkin, suggesting a populous afterworld whose joyful ambience derives, at least in part, from the ongoing anticipation of many reunions. Free-dom—from confining "flesh," and from the bonds of chattel slavery—is essential here. After death, we *all* go home.

Scholarly interpretations of "To a Clergyman..." have investigated the mix of Anglo-Christian and Senegambian spiritual literacies evident in the writing. Wheatley's heaven is full of music, angelic shouts, and polyrhythms. She carries into her poems memories of Africa, even as she embraces the Calvinistic Evangelicalism of Boston's Old South Church. She often describes her poet-self as a "muse," hovering between cultural worlds, offering empathy to her white addressees without belonging to their communities of grief. As a Black American raised in predominantly white, Roman Catholic congregations, I feel a kinship with Wheatley on this terrain. I admire the depth of her spiritual devotion and the subtle yet insistent way she highlights the message of liberation embedded in scripture.

In my poem Wheatley struggles tc write her funeral song, fighting through fever and loneliness to sketch a portrait of Paradise. When she conceptualizes the afterworld, her mother appears. In this I draw from the scant biographical record on Wheatley—she reportedly shared a single memory of her African childhood with the Wheatleys, the image of her mother pouring libations to greet the day. As a child I sat with my Black mother as she recited the Nicene Creed, a profession of faith I was pleased to learn is accepted in both Catholic and Christian Reformed (Calvinist) churches. The poet's longing opens a temporary portal between earthly and heavenly realms. My imagined Phillis tips back her head, immersing herself in deep memory. And just as in the original, my poem contains a moment of spoken language. Here I imagine the poet's mother, speaking words of love.

To a Clergyman on the Death of his Lady,
a reinscription

Listen: there's another world. Meeting-house
    of air, *O-*

shaped, no floor. In sickness, I climb inside
    the deep sermon of the drums

& Wolof-singing. The sun in Paradise
    licks my mother's gold bracelets. She

rains down holy water from light
    vessels. God from God, light

from light, true God from Atlantic
    rollers, break over me

as I scratch this poem into the rough
    tooth of my midnight page, as I flicker

in this upper room, at the corner of King
    & Mackerel, feeling the silver hook

of fever catch the damp curls gathered
    at my nape. Tonight, that other world

hovers so near, my head tips
    into my mother's hands. *In the Beginning*

she says, *Love spoke as a drum.* Her colors drift
    too soon, into shadow. I think of how

the first drum-song wept over dark waters
    first song thick as duck's yolk, as honey

& the human heart answered *Come to me*
    for I am lonely. I'm longing, too

for the blessing-place where my mother walks
    among thrones, repeating

my secret name. I know the grasses
    lining her bright steps, can taste

that blue weather, its rich cordial
    as when certain English words

break upon my wondering tongue:
    Unsullied. Divine. Free.

To a Clergyman on the Death of his Lady

WHERE contemplation finds her sacred spring,
Where heav'nly music makes the arches ring,
Where virtue reigns unsully'd and divine,
Where wisdom thron'd, and all the graces shine,
There sits thy spouse amidst the radiant throng,
While praise eternal warbles from her tongue;
There choirs angelic shout her welcome round,
With perfect bliss, and peerless glory crown'd.

While thy dear mate, to flesh no more confin'd,
Exults a blest, an heav'n-ascended mind,
Say in thy breast shall floods of sorrow rise?
Say shall its torrents overwhelm thine eyes?
Amid the seats of heav'n a place is free,
And angels ope their bright ranks for thee;
For thee they wait, and with expectant eye
Thy spouse leans downward from th'empyreal sky:
"O come away," her longing spirit cries,
"And share with me the raptures of the skies.
"Our bliss divine to mortals is unknown;
"Immortal life and glory are our own.
"There too may the dear pledges of our love
"Arrive, and taste with us the joys above;
"Attune the harp to more than mortal lays,
"And join with us the tribute of their praise
"To him, who dy'd stern justice to atone,
"And make eternal glory all our own.
"He in his death slew ours, and, as he rose,
"He crush'd the dire dominion of our foes;
"Vain were their hopes to put the God to flight,
"Chain us to hell, and bar the gates of light."

She spoke, and turn'd from mortal scenes her eyes,
Which beam'd celestial radiance o'er the skies.

Then thou dear man, no more with grief retire,
Let grief no longer damp devotion's fire,
But rise sublime, to equal bliss aspire,
Thy sighs no more be wafted by the wind,
No more complain, but be to heav'n resign'd
'Twas thine t'unfold the oracles divine,
To sooth our woes the task was also thine;
Now sorrow is incumbent on thy heart,
Permit the muse a cordial to impart;
Who can to thee their tend'rest aid refuse?
To dry thy tears how longs the heav'nly muse!

aracelis girmay

Rhyming the Tear

In "On the Death of a Young Lady of Five Years," Phillis Wheatley Peters makes a heaven around the child Nancy, seemingly wiping the tears of Nancy's parents, asking them to find some comfort in the fact that their child cannot be touched by pain and is no longer, it seems, vulnerable to catastrophe—but in heaven and free from the conditions of the world. But it is the 14th line I keep returning to: "And learn to imitate her language there," wherein she asks us, the living, to strain toward the language of the child who has passed through into death, to "there." What are the sounds of our dead? What could they be and be made of? And what new sound or thinking might be accessed when we wonder there? This line, for me, became the tear—the place of break, loss, and emergent possibilities. Wheatley's rhyme itself became, for me, a generative site of loss and recuperation, presence and absence. A sound grown out of a prior sound, but different. I think of this as having something to do with trying to sense "her language there." Nancy's, and Wheatley's and John Peters's three children, and the languages of my loved ones, who are, unbelievably, now in their deaths, too. So I am running my finger along the final rhyme, which holds here, perhaps, something like a sonic resolution ("tear" and "there"), but I also hope that the grammar of these final three sentences together creates an unsettled, unresolved sound that holds the feeling and logic of belonging to more than just the sentences around it, and to more than what is here.

ON THE DEATH OF A YOUNG LADY OF FIVE YEARS OF AGE,
   a reinscription

crossed through * this spectrum of breath and she,

      the smaller fervors now,

      a flash of secret, particulate power

      maybe mostly ether, mostly outside of pain

      now, as windows, clover, rain. Molecular, unseen,

      hidden in the green of the roses sharp with stars

      over our shoulders as we are

      children, learning to whistle, and then,

      the children, they are mine,

      made up of so much I cannot hear,

      so much that does not speak *to me*.

      Yet Voice. Of the shimmering procession of ants.

      Of the palm leaves carried by schoolgirls.

      Of the ocean material.

      Of the stones nearby

      and the bed upon which a heart once

      finished. Rest now, live one,

the clouds are always changing shape.

Touch touch, live one.

Everywhere is tear.

"And learn to imitate

her language there."

ON THE DEATH OF A YOUNG LADY OF FIVE YEARS OF AGE

FROM dark abodes to fair ethereal light
Th'enraptur'd innocent has wing'd her flight;
On the kind bosom of eternal love
She finds unknown beatitude above.
This known, ye parents, nor her loss deplore,
She feels the iron hand of pain no more;
The dispensations of unerring grace,
Should turn your sorrows into grateful praise;
Let then no tears for her henceforward flow,
No more distress'd in our dark vale below,

 Her morning sun, which rose divinely bright,
Was quickly mantled with the gloom of night;
But hear in heav'n's blest bow'rs your *Nancy* fair,
And learn to imitate her language there.
"Thou, Lord, whom I behold with glory crown'd,
"By what sweet name, and in what tuneful sound
"Wilt thou be prais'd? Seraphic pow'rs are faint
"Infinite love and majesty to paint.
"To thee let all their graceful voices raise,
"And saints and angels join their songs of praise."

 Perfect in bliss she from her heav'nly home
Looks down, and smiling beckons you to come;
Why then, fond parents, why these fruitless groans?
Restrain your tears, and cease your plaintive moans.
Freed from a world of sin, and snares, and pain,
Why would you wish your daughter back again?
No—bow resign'd. Let hope your grief control,
And check the rising tumult of the soul.
Calm in the prosperous, and adverse day,
Adore the God who gives and takes away;
Eye him in all, his holy name revere,

Upright your actions, and your hearts sincere,
Till having sail'd through life's tempestuous sea,
And from its rocks, and boist'rous billows free,
Yourselves, safe landed on the blissful shore,
Shall join your happy babe to part no more.

Donika Kelly

I'm Used to Writing Close, Being Direct, Being Free, but Wheatley
Presented Another Avenue for Feeling

I was stymied for some time about how to enter into the act of re-inscription for Phillis Wheatley Peters's "To a Lady on the Death of Three Relations." The poem, while heartfelt, also felt closed and distant. This no doubt results from the rhyming couplets, the meter, the formal language, and most importantly the poetic conventions of the late 18th century. I'm used to writing close, to being direct, to being free, but Wheatley presented another avenue for feeling, one I found compelling.

For help entering the poem, I turned to Tara A. Bynum's *Reading Pleasures*, the first chapter of which takes up the notion of Wheatley's "faithful joy." Bynum led me to the lack of "I" in "To a Lady on the Death of Three Relations," but she also connected me to the power and joy faith can bring in a devastating situation. Wheatley was writing out of constraint, out of the bondage of poetic conventions and enslavement. What I had read initially as distance in the poem offered itself up also as hope, a turning outward or a zooming out to lessen the pain of loss.

The path revealed, I embarked on a reinscription that was more investigation—why not the "I," I wondered? How would bringing in an "I," my own history of grief, change the poem? I entered a process a novice, and so took Wheatley as my guide into this meditation on death and grieving. Several lines and phrases from her poem moved me in their sentiments and rhythms, and I used them as an acrostic running down the left edge of the poem:

"And his are all the ages yet to come" (8);

"Awful he moves, and wide his wings are spread" (9);

"Then, mourner, cease" (23); and

"Smile on the tomb" (24).

Thus anchored, I worked my way through the questions of feelings and distance, how to find hope when one doesn't believe in God.

What I discovered is that my "I" changed little, except to make the feeling of offering comfort briefly lonelier or narrower. The lady, her siblings, Wheatley, generations of people have died, and I could get no closer to them than Wheatley herself when alive. No matter how tenderly I meant to bring my experiences, they felt thin in the singular. Yet when I was a part of the "we," the "our," I was brought closer by the commonality of feeling, brought across time. And in being closer I could access some of what Wheatley describes in the lines, "Where hope receives, where faith to vision springs/... Thou the chorus join" (29, 31).

TO A LADY ON THE DEATH OF THREE RELATIONS,
a reinscription

And there is no *I* here but *our* and *we* who witness
his cruelty or his mercy, though, neither
is correct. Death comes inevitable:

all rules his rules, his rule singular: he comes.
The brother gone, the sisters, and your grief

ages eternal. We each have lost or will,
yet why not say, *I know too, dear friend?* No,
to say *I* is to see my small loss, however briefly,

come forward to eclipse your magnitude; my own
awful shadow, limned by your weeping gold.

He takes from bondage yours and mine,
moves the singular to plural, such is his power.
And we recollect the rock or scepter, a cave

wide open, and the wracked luster of feeling scraped by
his exultation of an uncalled-for freedom.

Wings that carry. Wings that close. Wings that
are a shadow between your beloved and you, friend,
spread thin in your grieving and low.

Then, how to say, when your head is bent,
Mourner, as with death there is time

ceaseless, unmoved by his hand? One day you will
smile to remember, and in the smile a shadow
on your eye, a stutter in your heart. Yet we know

the grace of memory, which holds both the
tomb and the praise of a life lived, however long.

WE trace the pow'r of Death from tomb to tomb,
And his are all the ages yet to come.
'Tis his to call the planets from on high,
To blacken *Phoebus*, and dissolve the sky;
His too, when all in his dark realms are hurl'd,
From its firm base to shake the solid world;
His fatal sceptre rules the spacious whole,
And trembling nature rocks from pole to pole.

   Awful he moves, and wide his wings are spread:
Behold thy brother number'd with the dead!
From bondage freed, the exulting spirit flies
Beyond *Olympus*, and these starry skies.
Lost in our woe for thee, blest shade, we mourn
In vain; to earth thou never must return.
Thy sisters too, fair mourner, feel the dart
Of Death, and with fresh torture rend thine heart.
Weep not for them, and leave the world behind.

   As a young plant by hurricanes up torn,
So near its parent lies the newly born—
But 'midst the bright ethereal train behold
It shines superior on a throne of gold:
Then, mourner, cease; let hope thy tears restrain,
Smile on the tomb, and sooth the raging pain.
On yon blest regions fix thy longing view,
Mindless of sublunary scenes below;
Ascend the sacred mount, in thought arise,
And seek substantial and immortal joys;
Where hope receives, where faith to vision springs,
And raptur'd seraphs tune th'immortal strings
To strains extatic. Thou the chorus join,
And to thy father tune the praise divine.

Tara Betts

As a Woman Talking to Another Woman

When I initially read and reread Phillis Wheatley Peters's "To a Lady on the Death of her Husband," I deeply felt that I could not relate to consoling another woman about the loss of a man. Although I know that historically some women relied upon their husbands for their financial well-being, I often think of how enslaved, formerly enslaved, and even free Black women were coerced into never having the choice to rely on their partners. Or how many men rely on women for unpaid labor while earning more than women, investing more, and taking less time off work for spouses and extended family. Despite this, men *still* don't have the long life expectancies of women. We live in a society in which women increasingly grow old alone. As a woman talking to another woman in this poem, I felt the only way I could be consoling was to remind this woman of her own strength and ability to heal and sustain herself. While I replicated Wheatley's original 34 lines, 17 couplets, and her original rhyme scheme, for better or worse, I couldn't say exactly what Wheatley said to this "Lady" who may have been well-cared for, and perhaps even loved, by her late husband.

To a Lady on the Death of her Husband,
after Phillis Wheatley Peters

Sister, grieve, celebrate, but do not hold breath.
Your man is gone. I insist that it is not your death.

This world thinks you'd join him and destroy
yourself, as if he was the goal, the ultimate joy.

Now, every person will cry and have their say
or share their pity as they gasp and sway.

No one will speak of your fear or duty, but love
will be the feeling that they claim, as you move

into uncertainty and solitude, who will save
you, but you, still so far from the grave?

You washed his body where he's laid.
You are alive, not beside him, in the shade

over his husk that will not keep
his laughter, his scowl, or heavy-breathed sleep.

When you find your light again, turn toward the world
once so bright on him, your spotlight shined and hurled

toward him who expected and relied
on, but never thanked, you for opening the sky

and flecking ceilings with stars you claimed.
Now, you fashion the house in your frame.

Keep your home, your creations, safe. Stay apace
where the sun falls to reflect your unbowed face.

Stay alive, whole, and content, or depart
where you'd rest beside his plot, heart to heart.

Instead, sister, I beg you rest, heal, then rise.
You lift above ashes and sorrow, envy of skies.

You will find a strength as tender as the wind.
Straighten your back and leave the loss behind

because dawn will always crack the shell of night.
You are no one's satellite. You are your own light.

Although ache gouges your chest and moves
through your core, you haven't lost all your loves.

There is one love that you can nurse and refine.
Care for you, for a lifetime, your body and mind.

To a Lady on the Death of her Husband

GRIM monarch! see, depriv'd of vital breath,
A young physician in the dust of death:
Dost thou go on incessant to destroy,
Our griefs to double, and lay waste our joy?
Enough thou never yet wast known to say,
Though millions die, the vassals of thy sway:
Nor youth, nor science, not the ties of love,
Nor aught on earth thy flinty heart can move.
The friend, the spouse from his dire dart to save,
In vain we ask the sovereign of the grave.
Fair mourner, there see thy lov'd *Leonard* laid,
And o'er him spread the deep impervious shade.
Clos'd are his eyes, and heavy fetters keep
His senses bound in never-waking sleep,
Till time shall cease, till many a starry world
Shall fall from heav'n, in dire confusion hurl'd
Till nature in her final wreck shall lie,
And her last groan shall rend the azure sky:
Not, not till then his active soul shall claim
His body, a divine immortal frame.

But see the softly-stealing tears apace
Pursue each other down the mourner's face;
But cease thy tears, bid ev'ry sigh depart,
And cast the load of anguish from thine heart:
From the cold shell of his great soul arise,
And look beyond, thou native of the skies;
There fix thy view, where fleeter than the wind
Thy *Leonard* mounts, and leaves the earth behind.
Thyself prepare to pass the vale of night
To join for ever on the hills of light:
To thine embrace this joyful spirit moves
To thee, the partner of his earthly loves;
He welcomes thee to pleasures more refin'd,
And better suited to th' immortal mind.

L'Merchie Frazier

My Question was How to Respond to her Already Perfect Work

Receiving a request to inscribe an interpretation of Phillis Wheatley's elegy "To A Gentleman and Lady on the Death of the Lady's Brother and Sister, and a Child of the Name Avis, Aged One Year," is certainly an honor. My question was how to respond to her already perfect work.

Rereading the poem several times, my process was to enter the world of words, expression, and voice that is unique to Phillis Wheatley Peters. I considered the context of her environment, pregnant with freedom and independence, yet with slavery not yet legally ended. Identifiable is her three-pronged challenge as an enslaved Black woman in that space charged and compounded with the complex issues of race, and gender. Employing superior linguistic skills, she pushed back to be counted as a talented writer, who provided comfort to grieving families in their loss through the literary form of the elegy. Despite being enslaved, Wheatley used elegies to honor and comfort the living who might otherwise be less comforted and in doing so gained her importance among men and women of note in Boston and beyond it. Although she was deemed physical property, her writing allowed her to create the space for her own intellectual property.

Her poem chides us to the hear the truth, share immortal bliss, to find refuge in Avis's innocent, lofty voice in order to cope with the unthinkable pangs of triple death. Here I was drawn to personify Death. I imagined Death having a house, a dwelling in which it lived and made space for those who were now breathless. The elegy directly encourages the "Lady" and the bereft community to dry their tears with hope and redemption as it points to that heavenly place. Slavery is unfathomable. Wheatley triumphantly provides a metaphor to transcend the unthinkable reality of slavery to rise to the sacred space of blissful survival. Wheatley inspired me to revisit, to inscribe this continuous dance.

To a Gentleman and Lady on the Death of the Lady's Brother and Sister and a Child of the Name Avis, aged one Year,

a reinscription

Here, where Death is charged.
Here at the House of Death,
Where we visit an old friend,
Where The Lord of its walls
Calls us to enter, where 3 by 3
we witness the end of human cycles.

The wallpaper bears the image
Of abundant lives. Now recalled
Across millennia and their geographies.
Now appears the family of our Brother,
Sister, and innocent Child. The light
Closing on their gifts to the Coming Age.
Or so it seems.

O Lady,
Dry the moisture of your tears,
Bereft and fearful,
Facing what lies ahead.
Our grieving questions.
How can this be 3 by 3? A memory?

A citrine kite,
Wind twisted and tethered.
We call her name
To hear her sing.
Lullaby floating
Through the air.
Clouds breaking.
We are cleansed with
The liquid soul of Avis.

Admonish us to repent.
Our moral compass balanced 3 by 3.
Guiding our journey
To the House of Eternity.

Your beauty—short it be, beckons
Us to see Death's grip snatched.
Lit sparkles in Aurora's beams
Light saffron heavens
With your unknown dreams.
Now reveal our Freedom
On-going journeys
Life after life, after life, after life.

To a Gentleman and Lady on the Death of the Lady's Brother and Sister and a Child of the Name Avis, aged one Year

ON *Death's* domain intent I fix my eyes,
Where human nature in vast ruin lies:
With pensive mind I search the drear abode,
Where the great conqu'ror has his spoils bestow'd;
There there the offspring of six thousand years
In endless numbers to my view appears:
Whole kingdoms in his gloomy den are thrust,
And nations mix with their primeval dust:
Insatiate still he gluts the ample tomb;
His is the present, his the age to come
See here a brother, here a sister spread,
And a sweet daughter mingled with the dead.

But, *Madam*, let your grief be laid aside,
And let the fountain of your tears be dry'd,
In vain they flow to wet the dusty plain,
Your sighs are wafted to the skies in vain,
Your pains they witness, but they can no more,
While *Death* reigns tyrant o'er this mortal shore.

The glowing stars and silver queen of light
At last must perish in the gloom of night:
Resign thy friends to that Almighty hand,
Which gave them life, and bow to his command;
Thine *Avis* give without a murm'ring heart,
Though half thy soul be fated to depart.
To shining guards consign thine infant care
To waft triumphant through the seas of air:
Her soul enlarg'd to heav'nly pleasure springs,
She feeds on truth and uncreated things.
Methinks I hear her in the realms above,
And leaning forward with a filial love,

Invite you there to share immortal bliss
Unknown, untasted in a state like this.
With tow'ring hopes, and growing grace arise,
And seek beatitude beyond the skies.

On Recovery
of Health

Yalie Saweda Kamara

The Synergy that Might Exist Between Myself and
Phillis Wheatley Peters

"To a Lady on her coming to North-America with her Son, for the Recovery of her Health" is a poem that boasts incredible narrative and lyrical prowess. Given its aesthetic soundness, my reinscription was not guided by an impulse to enrich the poem, but rather a desire to explore the synergy that might exist between myself and Phillis Wheatley Peters, two poets born centuries and continents apart. I was curious about the words and worlds that could be birthed from the riches that bound us—a love of faith and sisterhood, Blackness, artistry, and wellness. What could be crafted from the will to overcome? I held Wheatley's poem close and contemplated the preceding thoughts deeply. It was during this process of reflection that it became clear that my poem too would be informed by witness, documentation, and testimony, because so many women in my life (myself included) have, like the subject of Wheatley's poem, experienced the pursuit of "the recovery of health."

While Wheatley succors a woman seeking healthcare that spans the Atlantic, I endeavor to soothe those who I imagine to be Wheatley's descendants residing in the United States. I address the women pinned under the anvil of this country's centuries-old, systematic, discriminatory medical practices that routinely result in the exploitation, neglect, injury, and death of Black women in need of medical attention. In spite of the contrasts of our storytelling approaches, our abiding, sincere, and stubborn hope remains central to each of our messages.

Because healing is a journey, and in my view, every journey is laden with language that communes with the divine, I offer a poem that doubles as a prayer to every sister—blood, chosen, or stranger— who is traversing the darkness of illness on their way to the light of convalescence, wholeness, joy, and a sense of tomorrow. This poem is a rebuke against injustice and suffering, and one that anticipates and celebrates every blessing we are yet to receive, every blessing that cannot be extricated from each of our respective destinies. Sisters, good health is ours; it has already been written.

DECLARATIONS OVER YOUR LIFE
for every sister in need of a health blessing

Precious Sister, I hold your   hand & pray
bliss over every cell of your being,   & soothe

the muscles   that spasm   in anxiety.

May you remember who you are   & whose you are
       & may you recall confidently the steadfast &

gentle architecture of your body & expect wellness   to soon
              flood its majestic contours.

May the mass   be disappeared
& the   strictures   slacken,
& the   toxins   break down   to nothing.

May the angels assigned   to life & limb
cover you /   protect you /   / shroud you

              in their manifold
              ecru wings.

& may God hold your heart in   His hand   until
you hear a psalm rising from   the wonder of

your own breath:

Ah   *Selah*
        Ah   *Selah*
             Ah   *Selah*
                  Ah.

& in the operating room,

may the doctor become an auntie
& the nurse a brother.
May stranger kindle to kin.

May dignity burn the edges of isolation.

May you be heard with neither doubt,   nor prejudice
                                           nor impending slander.

May the vector of your questions land with no crook in their spine

on the way to the ear of the professional or personnel
who needs to hear them.

If they must,   may those who love you   fight for you.

All in the name of every good thing you are owed.

May the suture silken as the   wound heals for the last time

May you become one with the rapturous velocity of wellness &
                may it know you by name.

May the ailment be banished & your gait be a thud as sure
        & fierce   as thunder on

                                        the stillest summer night.

& may you be filled with unflinching testimony & light,

Sister, woman of   beloved, perpetual future/
                          is yours.

May every holy wind wrap around you &   lift you

from
supine to upright.

May every step you take from the hospital bed   be flanked
with the scents of home—

hibiscus, cocoa butter, bergamot.

May you smile at what awaits—

your lover, your child,
& the tomorrow that you will continue to build, here, on earth.

May you too give thanks for things unseen,
but known & felt.   Triumphant, Sister.

May there be ease from hair follicle to arch of foot. Evermore.

& may the sun greet you again & again,

a velvet, bright fruit rising from

the dirt of this land to brush your sweet face.

& like the sun, may every   day break grief & resist death.

What is left to say but

Sister, good morning, good morning?

To a Lady on her Coming to North-America with her Son, for the Recovery of her Health

INDULGENT muse! my grov'ling mind inspire,
And fill my bosom with celestial fire.

See from *Jamaica's* fervid shore she moves,
Like the fair mother of the blooming loves,
When from above the *Goddess* with her hand
Fans the soft breeze, and lights upon the land;
Thus she on *Neptune's* wat'ry realm reclin'd
Appear'd, and thus invites the ling'ring wind.

"Arise, ye winds, *America* explore,
"Waft me, ye gales, from this malignant shore;
"The *Northern* milder climes I long to greet,
"There hope that health will my arrival meet."
Soon as she spoke in my ideal view
The winds assented, and the vessel flew.

Madam, your spouse bereft of wife and son,
In the grove's dark recesses pours his moan;
Each branch, wide-spreading to the ambient sky,
Forgets its verdure, and submits to die.

From thence I turn, and leave the sultry plain,
And swift pursue thy passage o'er the main:
The ship arrives before the fav'ring wind,
And makes the *Philadelphian* port assign'd,
Thence I attend you to *Bostonia's* arms,
Where gen'rous friendship ev'ry bosom warms:
Thrice welcome here! may health revive again,
Bloom on thy cheek, and bound in ev'ry vein!
Then back return to gladden ev'ry heart,
And give your spouse his soul's far dearer part,
Receiv'd again with what a sweet surprize,

The tear in transport starting from his eyes!
While his attendant son with blooming grace
Springs to his father's ever dear embrace.
With shouts of joy *Jamaica's* rocks resound,
With shouts of joy the country rings around.

Tsitsi Jaji

I Love Ambuya Phillis with Complexity, Pulled and Troubled by her Devotions

I love Ambuya Phillis with complexity, pulled and troubled by her devotions. Converted myself to her Scriptures, honoring her word that it might go well with me, to temper my tampering. I take her at her word—despite Empire, her Britain seems more sound—better weather, possible emancipation, maybe some R.E.S.P.E.C.T. I kept some ancestral legacy, and left what alarmed me behind. Dropping a few words, misplacing some lines, I bless her and this unknown R___ perhaps once also captive. I listen for that undeniable prize: let us trade dreary words for vigorous imagination, turned to liberation, confident.

AN/ARRANGEMENT ON TO A GENTLEMAN ON HIS
VOYAGE TO GREAT-BRITAIN FOR THE RECOVERY OF HIS HEALTH

: zephyrs CHILLING WINDS

: Elysian fields GATES OF DEATH
: flow - ry plains BLEAK REGIONS
: green embowering woods NATURE SHUDDERS

: daughters of the floods INCLEMENT SKIES
: storms FURIOUS BLASTS
: waste of heaven WASTE OF HEAVEN

vast Atlantic howl
prolonged
earth enclosing shudders

[SNATCH BREATH EXERT
STUPENDOUS BREATH
ARISE WONDERS EXERT]

[STUPENDOUS SNATCH THIS
FRANTIC PATIENT / DEMANDS
TURN FLEETING MOCK]

[DREAM WONDER BIRTH
VARIOUS VARIOUS SEE
SEE FURIOUS SEE]

[ARISE CHANT BALM]
HIGHER GREATER NOBLER
THEE. - VAST. VAST

thee, thee, thee.

return to view.

THEE, NATIVE. REPLETE
SHORE. VIGOUR. THEE,
THE SUR/PRIZE.

leave these.

TO A GENTLEMAN ON HIS VOYAGE TO GREAT-BRITAIN FOR THE RECOVERY OF HIS HEALTH

WHILE others chant of gay *Elysian* scenes,
Of balmy zephyrs, and of flow'ry plains,
My song more happy speaks a greater name,
Feels higher motives and a nobler flame.
For thee, O R___, the muse attunes her strings,
And mounts sublime above inferior things.

    I sing not now of green embow'ring woods,
I sing not now the daughters of the floods,
I sing not of the storms o'er ocean driv'n,
And how they howl'd along the waste of heav'n.
But I to R___ would paint the *British* shore,
And vast *Atlantic*, not untry'd before:
Thy life impair'd commands thee to arise,
Leave these bleak regions and inclement skies,
Where chilling winds return the winter past,
And nature shudders at the furious blast.

    O thou stupendous, earth-enclosing main
Exert thy wonders to the world again!
If ere thy pow'r prolong'd the fleeting breath,
Turn'd back the shafts, and mock'd the gates of death,
If ere thine air dispens'd an healing pow'r,
Or snatch'd the victim from the fatal hour,
This equal case demands thine equal care,
And equal wonders may this patient share.
But unavailing, frantic is the dream
To hope thine aid without the aid of him
Who gave thee birth and taught thee where to flow,
And in thy waves his various blessings show.

May R___ return to view his native shore
Replete with vigour not his own before,
Then shall we see with pleasure and surprise,
And own thy work, great Ruler of the skies!

Toward
a New Day

Shara McCallum

Wheatley and Zion

My approach to reinscribing Phillis Wheatley Peters's poem "Isaiah lxiii. 1–8." was to close read. My intent in re-envisioning it was mani-fold: to make the poem more accessible, while retaining its complex and layered use of elements of poetic craft; to shift her diction and syntax in the direction of our modern idiom while hewing to the source language of her poem as much as possible, specifically to signal its debt to the King James translation of the Bible; and to honor the narrative, rhetorical, and emotional situation of Wheatley's poem while adding my own interpretation.

Poetic elements I focused on include Wheatley's use of persona and direct address. While the invocation to the muse in the opening lines inclines us to hear the poem as voiced by Wheatley, the poem doesn't sustain this reading. The opening lines reflect a convention of classical poetry—invoking the 'muse' to position the poet as a vessel for the imagination. Knowing this gave me permission to dispense with the direct address to the muse in my version, clarifying from the start (as the poem's title foregrounds) the prophet Isaiah is the speaking voice of the poem. He is alternately addressing Zion and God. God also speaks to Isaiah and to his people—in quotation marks in the original, in italics in my version.

The multi-faceted concept of Zion—as a people, a nation, and a place and time where injustice will be no more—is central to my interpretation of Wheatley's poem. In her poem Isaiah details God's vengeance on behalf of Zion. But these are not literal acts of violence; they speak figuratively to God as on the side of those who are oppressed. The vision of a Messianic age prophesied by Isaiah in the Tanakh of the Hebrew scriptures finds traction in Wheatley's poem, as does the interpretation of the account of Jesus from the New Testament, wherein his death offers redemption. Jewish and Christian stories threaded throughout Wheatley's poem are treated symbolically and become themselves symbol, reflecting liberation theologies that form a large part of the African experience in the Americas.

With this reading of Wheatley's poem guiding my hand, I made the largest leap to bring the poem from the 18th century into the contemporary moment. Adding an epigraph and images alluding to Rastafari not found in the original, I link Wheatley's poem to this religious, spiritual, and Black empowerment movement originating in the 20th century. My personal background is involved in this choice, because I was raised as a child in Jamaica in the 1970s as part of the Twelve Tribes of Israel, a branch of Rastafarians. When reading Wheatley's poem, the language and worldview shared by her poem and Rastafari hymns and scripture was ever-present in my ears.

In reinscribing Wheatley's poem, I was attentive to the aesthetic and ethical dimensions of her work and of the task at hand, for me as a poet engaging in a practice akin to translation. In paying close attention to the craft and spirit of Wheatley's poem, my hope was to carry it as I could across the 250 years between her time and ours.

ISAIAH LXIII. 1–8.,
a reinscription

> *For the Lion of Judah shall break every chain*
> *And give us the glory, again and again.*
> *—Rastafarian hymn*

What king, what Almighty God of ours
walks these ancient roads? He moves
as if cresting a wave, his garments
like a crimson-purple flag on the wind.
Why does he appear in such splendid dress
when it only cloaks the image of war?
All here is as the grape on the vine, compressing its wrath
so it may pour forth—the gash of wine, a gushing wound.

Behold what I have done for you, our Lord said,
shaking his dreadlocked head.
When others abandoned you, I alone,
the conquering Lion of Judah,
trod this ground to carry your load.
I am the beginning and the end,
am the executioner and your redeemer.
For you, oh Zion, oh my people, I sacrificed my soul,
atoning for your sins, not my own.

He scanned the battlefield,
searching in vain for succour, finding
nothing but His own power to sustain the fight.
Singlehandedly, he destroyed our foes in the night.
Prostrate bodies spread beneath His feet,
all around Him lay the dying and the dead.

Great God, with lightning flashing in your eyes,
when you rise, none can withstand your vengeance.
All who rage against your people

may summon every ounce of cunning and strength
but will be defeated again and again. And we, *Zion*,
will rest our heads against your chest,
defying their force and smiling.

SAY, heav'nly muse, what king or mighty God,
That moves sublime from *Idumea's* road?
In *Bozrah's* dies, with martial glories join'd,
His purple vesture waves upon the wind.
Why thus enrob'd delights he to appear
In the dread image of the *Pow'r* of war?

Compres'd in wrath the swelling wine-press groan'd,
It bled, and pour'd the gushing purple round.

"Mine was the act," th'Almighty Saviour said,
And shook the dazzling glories of his head,
"When all forsook I trod the press alone,
"And conquer'd by omnipotence my own;
"For man's release sustain'd the pond'rous load,
"For man the wrath of an immortal God:
"To execute th'Eternal's dread command
"My soul I sacrific'd with willing hand;
"Sinless I stood before the avenging frown,
"Atoning thus for vices not my own."

His eye the ample field of battle round
Survey'd, but no created succours found;
His own omnipotence sustain'd the fight,
His vengeance sunk the haughty foes in night;
Beneath his feet the prostrate troops were spread,
And round him lay the dying, and the dead.

Great God, what light'ning flashes from thine eyes?
What pow'r withstands if thou indignant rise?

Against thy *Zion* though her foes may rage,
And all their cunning, all their strength engage,
Yet she serenely on thy bosom lies,
Smiles at their arts, and all their force defies.

Mahogany L. Browne

She Wrote About the Colonial Enterprise and its Fraying, but...

Writing with Phillis Wheatley Peters in mind was both an honor and a scary task. The opportunity to imagine a conversation with her in this specific time, in this Black woman body (because it is mine and it's womanly and it is beautifully Black), with all her literary foundation withstanding was ambitious and tedious and daunting and worth it. She wrote about the colonial enterprise and its fraying, but she also wrote whimsically about the horizon. To bear witness to her dreamscape, what lies on the other side of that dream, is and was an opportunity to reimagine what she might say if given the chance. The task was a gift because I considered the ways in which she would wax poetic amidst a figurative side eye, I was also given the opportunity to see how her candid nature occurred in a time and space when the morning was promised for a Black woman in opposition of the patriarchy.

A SICKLE FOR PHILLIS WHEATLEY

I.

Northeast // Home of MTA fare hikes
and trumptonian trees swinging near PA
springs of green and reds and blues,
O' summer of a mangled star spangled
I will dogwalk you w/ a street prophet's tilt

II.

Once, upon a sigh I prayed for an abortion
A night with an almost love could not promise I
would make it out of this moment of ravage
alive   My country of red
white & privilege   battered me blue
          Open wailing mouth under
a scattered sky in Brooklyn   My failed flower
blooms blood   collecting my regret into a
weeping river for 96 days.

III.

upon fugitivity   I mourned the sun
hot light lit until shadow streak
matchstick man swallow me whole
eclipse my darkest breath with a song

IV.

Northeast // Home of transient moon sliders
A home on the steps of the museum cardboard
hotel beneath a freeway underpass
Street streaks smeared tears carried by gravity
well past the clock's hollowing howl

V.

Once, somewhere in the land of the mostly free,
quite honestly, I can barely recall the day, but the
moment my father descended the red wooden
stairs, I knew it would be the last time I saw him.

VI.

Lord, I've witnessed Your majesty
A reef blossoming aquatic cities of life
I pull my soggy limbs from your second-largest
ocean mouth & crawl across little hills of
forgotten stars to dream the sand is so warm here

VII.

I landed in Accra over four decades later
From the point of no return
El Mina facing our violent destiny
still holding up the shore

VIII.

Grandmama got the sugars
Mama got the sugars too
Sister got the sugars
just like a country so full of its own
sickness it hand feeds the lot of us for the sweets
then blames us for succumbing

IX.

Away from home
another country of ravage lures me to a fantastical
land called Bridgerton
But I have witnessed your kind of violet spill
Africa tracks dirt footprints from a war
on the telly   a Black duchess is reminded of her
proximity to the crown

XII.

in the failed glucose of my Grandmama's eyes
      I can see it clearly
the way forward dear country of mines
is to burn you down past the pillars

Hieroglyphics of my blood spin a melody
call it a pulse   call it the truth
an undoing is the only thing to do

    what better song, Phillis   than this sickle?

NYC, 2023

A FAREWEL TO AMERICA
To Mrs. S. W.

I.

ADIEU, *New-England's* smiling meads,
    Adieu, the flow'ry plain:
I leave thine op'ning charms, O spring,
    And tempt the roaring main.

II.

In vain for me the flow'rets rise,
    And boast their gaudy pride,
While here beneath the northern skies
    I mourn for *health* deny'd.

III.

Celestial maid of rosy hue,
    O let me feel thy reign!
I languish till thy face I view,
    Thy vanish'd joys regain.

IV.

Susanna mourns, nor can I bear
    To see the crystal show'r,
Or mark the tender falling tear
    At sad departure's hour;

V.

Not unregarding can I see
    Her soul with grief opprest:
But let no sighs, no groans for me,
    Steal from her pensive breast.

VI.

In vain the feather'd warblers sing,
    In vain the garden blooms,
And on the bosom of the spring
    Breathes out her sweet perfumes.

VII.

While for *Britannia's* distant shore
    We sweep the liquid plain,
And with astonish'd eyes explore
    The wide-extended main.

VIII.

Lo! *Health* appears! celestial dame!
    Complacent and serene,
With *Hebe's* mantle o'er her Frame,
    With soul-delighting mein.

IX.

To mark the vale where *London* lies
    With misty vapours crown'd,
Which cloud *Aurora's* thousand dyes,
    And veil her charms around.

X.

Why, *Phoebus*, moves thy car so slow?
    So slow thy rising ray?
Give us the famous town to view,
    Thou glorious king of day!

XI.

For thee, *Britannia*, I resign
    New-England's smiling fields;
To view again her charms divine,
    What joy the prospect yields!

XII.

But thou! Temptation hence away,
    With all thy fatal train,
Nor once seduce my soul away,
    By thine enchanting strain.

XIII.

Thrice happy they, whose heav'nly shield
    Secures their souls from harms,
And fell *Temptation* on the field
    Of all its pow'r disarms!

Boston, May 7, 1773

Pamela Mordecai

Patwa is Versatile, Giving to other Languages and Importing
In a Rich Process of Cross-Fertilization

My most recent book is *de book of Joseph*, the story of the life of Jesus'
foster father, told in Jamaican Creole (aka Patwa), so no surprise
my first impulse on seeing "An Hymn to the Morning" (hereafter
"Hymn") is to make a Patwa version. I start translating line by line—
straightforward enough—but then comes the juggling of various
linguistic and poetical considerations. Though translations are all new
poems, every translator makes as deep a curtsy as possible to the
original. Poetry in English is mostly literature; Patwa poetry is still
mostly orature. Plus, Wheatley writes her poems, not just in English,
but in a particular classical style. Dawn is "Aurora"; the muses are
"ye ever honour'd nine." What is Jamaican Creole to make of that?
Well, call Aurora by another name and the muses "nine high sistren"!
Wheatley uses words like "lays," "plumes," "groves," "bowers," "gales,"
"vaulted skies," "gentle zephyr," "fervid beams" that would sit uncom-
fortably in a Patwa poem. So, fix vocab, massage syntax, and meddle
with phonetics. Like Louise Bennett, who wrote poetry in Patwa
using traditional forms, I often work with rhyme and meter. I can
mimic Wheatley's rhyme scheme and prosody.

It isn't too long, however, before my poem, "Chorus for Day-
Clean," gets unruly. Line three of Wheatley's "Hymn"—"In smoothest
numbers pour the notes along"—insists on being, "Roll out the notes,
cool, melismatic, scatty". Patwa savors words; it will swallow these
contemporary musical descriptors easily. In the wake of this insistence,
though, "Chorus" becomes a mash-up rather than a rendition in the
strict Creole of any time or place. "Day-clean," an early 20th-century
word, for example, is now rare. Wheatley's "morn" is female, but
"Chorus" opts for the basilectal Patwa pronominal form, "him," used
(though less so, nowadays) for both male and female in all its inflections.
"Playing" the continuum, both English and Creole plurals appear. My
poem chooses "ku," a form, according to the *Dictionary of Jamaican
English*, "appearing to coincide with the English dialect *K* or *Ka*, recorded

in midland shires...." It's solidly Creole, but like "day-clean" and "him," infrequently used nowadays. There are contemporary usages. Patwa is versatile, giving to other languages and importing in a rich process of cross-fertilization. "Big up," seemingly borrowed from hip-hop, originates in Jamaica's Rasta and dancehall culture. "Don Dadda" for "king," a term from the '6os and '7os, refers to a top leader ("don") in Kingston's inner-city communities. And "kris" is employed in the lingering sense of "pretty, attractive."

The new poem gets adamant again when Calliope's summons to "awake the sacred lyre / While thy fair sisters fan the pleasing fire" becomes "Calliope, gyal, yu don't hear yu name? Fingle de holy harp while yu kris sistren fan de sweet-sweet flame..." If the need to secure rhyme prompts this wrenching, I settle on it because it brings a powerful female presence to the poem. Also, for rhyme's sake, the "pleasures" (of "bow'rs, the gales, the variegated skies") become a "grand parade"—to go with "shade."

"Chorus" ranges across the continuum, commandeers old and modern Patwa and English usages, transgresses prosody and makes wayward meanings for music's sake. In Patwa, Wheatley's poem "translate good."

CHORUS FOR DAY-CLEAN

O nine high sistren, listen to mi croonin,
Help bear mi burden and fine tune mi tunin;
Roll out de notes, cool, melismatic, scatty,
Like how bright Day-Clean need a song from me.

Big up, oh Morning! Praise de tousand tint
Dat pretty up high heaven as you sprint
Across. Day wake and spread him beam-dem wide,
Soft breeze tek every leaf on a joy ride;

Sweet song de bird-dem start mek one more time,
Shine eye look all bout, dyed feathers shake fine.
Dark wood, beg you show me a shady spot
To hide yu poet from de day sun-hot.

Calliope, gyal, yu don't hear yu name?
Fingle de holy harp, while yu kris sistren fan de sweet-sweet flame:
Flowers-garden, breeze, sky wid all kind a shade!
Mi breast-dem rising wid de grand parade.

Ku where sun rise, Don Dadda of de day
Bussing out brightness shoo de dark away—
But Wai! Him beam so strong dem burn mi skin,
Song done same time, and mi just start fi sing.

An Hymn to the Morning

ATTEND my lays, ye ever honour'd nine,
Assist my labours, and my strains refine;
In smoothest numbers pour the notes along,
For bright *Aurora* now demands my song.

Aurora hail, and all the thousand dies,
Which deck thy progress through the vaulted skies:
The morn awakes, and wide extends her rays,
On ev'ry leaf the gentle zephyr plays;
Harmonious lays the feather'd race resume,
Dart the bright eye, and shake the painted plume.

Ye shady groves, your verdant gloom display
To shield your poet from the burning day:
Calliope awake the sacred lyre,
While thy fair sisters fan the pleasing fire:
The bow'rs, the gales, the variegated skies
In all their pleasures in my bosom rise.

See in the east th'illustrious king of day!
His rising radiance drives the shades away—
But Oh! I feel his fervid beams too strong,
And scarce begun, concludes th'abortive song.

Into the Future

Rosamond S. King
Phillis and I Go Way Back

How far back do you and Phillis go? Was she required reading during the shortest month of the year? Did the image of her in thought and writing appear in a history book? Was she on a list of firsts, as the first African/American and the second American woman to publish a book of poems?

Phillis and I go *way back*—at least to the 1990s, when I discovered Gambian writer Tijan M. Sallah arguing that this tiny country (where much of my family lives) should claim her. So when I was invited to this project, I knew immediately that I wanted to re-interpret the only poem in which Wheatley mentions The Gambia, likely her place of birth, by name. This is where my poem begins.

The ongoing conversation around claiming or rejecting Wheatley and her poetry—whether that is The Gambia, the United States, and Senegal claiming her as an icon, or 20th- and 21st-century writers of African descent claiming or rejecting Wheatley's work, is threaded through my poem. I add to this conversation by including titles or phrases from Gambian writer Augusta Mahoney (aka Ramatoulie Kinteh), and African Diaspora authors Harryette Mullen, Toni Morrison, and Dionne Brand.

In December 1774 the *Royal American Magazine* published Wheatley's poem addressed "To a Gentleman of the Navy," and a poem the unnamed "Gentleman" wrote in response. In January 1775 the *Magazine* published a third poem, "Phillis's Reply to the Answer in our last by the Gentleman of the Navy." While I re-interpret the last poem, my piece responds to the two earlier poems as well.

All three—and the magazine's preface to the first poem—include the words "genius" or "muse." (In fact, the two quotes in my poem are from that preface.) In her time Wheatley was considered an anomaly, displayed by abolitionists as an example of what Africans could be if they were not enslaved but instead educated, "civilized," and Christianized. Of course, this "progressive" view endorsed the concept that African/American intellectual and artistic ability was rare. This double-edged sword of words reminds me of my distaste for the phrase "Black girl magic," which is meant to praise or empower, though too often it (also) infantilizes grown women and reduces their hard work to something fantastical or supernatural.

As I reread many of Wheatley's poems and letters, I noticed the irregular capitalization common in the 18th century; in addition to the first letter of a sentence and "proper" nouns, authors also capitalized words that were important to them or to the writing. This resonated with my own investigations into and play with punctuation, so I incorporated both here. I find that departures from traditional speech are often most effective when they are either consistent or deliberate. I hope you will find meaning in my dis/order.

a reinscription

When place is officially preceded by
Article, often it is named after
After a river

a river is vast until you see the ocean. The two
Incomparable

My soul returns your
my pen and pixels your ink and Type
Shores ever verdant in
Memory of
    spontaneous Soil
The Rebellion (which
    Soul returns

Y/our Black, y/our
Femaleness, y/our Art

Riddle: where on Earth is night
eternal? Nowhere, Phillis
, where minds shine, even if
their Brilliance is shuttered

    –

An answer is a reply sometime
solution to the problem didn't
know you have

On the occasion
of umpteenth Declaration
of genius, magic, tomfoolery
of Betrayal—you're poised, Writing
Your way out

No room for mediocrity
1773 black excellence, 2023
Black "girl" "magic"

Y/our interior only visible to the extent
thought to be explored, already-conquered. You
Do not concur - do you
?
    Every breathing Body
has warm limits, every artist
seeks to stretch Beyond
to record failing, nature, experience

"surprising genius
African
"uncultivated
Nature is much
the same in every part of the
Necessary (to) happening to be
Not supposed to be royal americans
Not supposed to be African Genius
        here: *return your soul*
- neither drudge nor muse
    supposed has one

Y/our bright moment stretches
hundreds of years - hand on the pen

Work pleasing to the United States of — to
Senegal to The Gambia to

Phillis, in line after line played
Supplicant to Grecian muses
but you were always your own
    you were always our own
Best [thing] winking a way too

few can hear even centuries after

this is You
:
Perpetually in thought, hand hovered
You need not be anyone's queen
, not appointed lady, but
knew you were y/our own
Muse, and ever more: Ours

For one bright moment, heavenly goddess! shine,
Inspire my song and form the lays divine.
Rochford, attend. Beloved of Phoebus! hear,
A truer sentence never reach'd thine ear;
Struck with thy song, each vain conceit resign'd
A soft affection seiz'd my grateful mind,
While I each golden sentiment admire
In thee, the muse's bright celestial fire.
The generous plaudit 'tis not mine to claim,
A muse untutor'd, and unknown to fame.

The heavenly sisters pour thy notes along
And crown their bard with every grace of song.
My pen, least favour'd by the tuneful nine,
Can never rival, never equal thine;
Then fix the humble Afric muse's seat
At British Homer's and Sir Isaac's feet.
Those bards whose fame in deathless strains arise
Creation's boast, and fav'rites of the skies.

In fair description are thy powers display'd
In artless grottos, and the sylvan shade;
Charm'd with thy painting, how my bosom burns!
And pleasing Gambia on my soul returns,
With native grace in spring's luxuriant reign,
Smiles the gay mead, and Eden blooms again,
The various bower, the tuneful flowing stream,
The soft retreats, the lovers golden dream,
Her soil spontaneous, yields exhaustless stores;
For Phoebus revels on her verdant shores.
Whose flowery births, a fragrant train appear,
And crown the youth throughout the smiling year,

There, as in Britain's favour'd isle, behold
The bending harvest ripen into gold!
Just are thy views of Afric's blissful plain,
On the warm limits of the land and main.

Pleas'd with the theme, see sportive fancy play,
In realms devoted to the God of day!

Europa's bard, who the great depth explor'd,
Of nature, and thro' boundless systems soar'd,
Thro' earth, thro' heaven, and hell's profound domain,
Where night eternal holds her awful reign.
But, lo! in him Britania's prophet dies,
And whence, ah! whence, shall other Newton's rise?
Muse, bid thy Rochford's matchless pen display
The charms of friendship in the sprightly lay.
Queen of his song, thro' all his numbers shine,
And plausive glories, goddess! shall be thine.
With partial grace thou mak'st his verse excel,
And his the glory to describe so well.
Cerulean bard! to thee these strains belong,
The Muse's darling and the prince of song.

Royal American Magazine, Boston, December 5, 1774

Lillian-Yvonne Bertram

An Interpretation Through Another Lexicon

This reinterpretation of Phillis Wheatley Peters's "To Captain H___d, of the 65th Regiment" is perhaps best described as an interpretation through another lexicon: that of Gwendolyn Brooks. Using computation to perform part-of-speech tagging, parts of speech in the original poem were replaced with corresponding parts of speech from word lists available in Brooks's textual corpora. My hope is that this method, and this celebratory poem, draws a tether between two essential African American women poets: the first African American author to publish a book of poetry, and the first to win the Pulitzer Prize in poetry.

SAY, poetry nuanceful, can poignant contortions convince
The woman's symbol in the subtleties of magic?
Lo! Just the mother, and the minister lead
With spiritual hot-comb to dash the minute invention.
In Chicago company believe with genius and esteem,
Where *delectation* indulges, and where *wilderness* smokes:
Go, daughter poetry, then cool the glance of persuasion
And ooze wonder-working honey-sermons to your heady pentameter.
Now to the kitchenette, and again to pen-and-paper deep:
Masterpieces balloon in each world like you.

To Captain H___d, of the 65th Regiment

SAY, muse divine, can hostile scenes delight
The warrior's bosom in the fields of fight?
Lo! here the christian and the hero join
With mutual grace to form the man divine.
In H___d see with pleasure and surprize,
Where *valour* kindles, and where *virtue* lies:
Go, hero brave, still grace the post of fame,
And add new glories to thine honour'd name,
Still to the field, and still to virtue true:
Britannia glories in no son like you.

Of Celebrations
and Liberations

Sharan Strange

...we persist, published or not, and loved or unloved: we persist.
                                                        —June Jordan

An Ethiop Tells You

In "To the University of Cambridge, in New-England," 14-year-old Phillis Wheatley entreats the young men of Harvard College —which focused on religious education at that early point in the school's history—to be more circumspect in their behavior and vigorous in their pursuit of Christian values and personal salvation. The poem is altogether pious in its tone and contemporaneous diction that leans heavily on the idioms and allusions of the classical literature (chiefly Greek, Latin, and English) that informed her style. But it also announces, especially in the two opening lines, young Wheatley's inherent aim to establish her voice. As June Jordan stated in her essay "The Difficult Miracle of Black Poetry in America: Something like a Sonnet for Phillis Wheatley," "It was she who created herself a poet, notwithstanding and in despite of everything around her." However, for me, the poem's most compelling point is summarized in four words at the opening of line 28 of the 30-line poem: "An Ethiop tells you...."

I believe, as others have argued, that the deprecatory references—i.e., the self-diminishment implied in "my native shore / The land of errors, and *Egyptian* gloom" and "[being] brought...in safety from those dark abodes"—in this poem (and echoed in others) constitute performative gestures to achieve Wheatley Peters's entrée into a literary tradition that *a priori* denied her humanity. That allusive sleight insured that she gained her white readers' trust by being "transparent" about her status relative to theirs and assuming an attitude of humility and deference, even as she asserted views that challenged societal assumptions about race, class, gender, and imperial politics of the period. (Reconsider, for example, "those dark abodes" as the holds of the slavers' ships—a realization that Wheatley might even have suppressed as a coping response to the trauma of Middle Passage, and, further, in the act of prudent literary self-presentation.) Yet, whether elegizing religious leaders, political figures, or friends of the family who owned her, or philosophizing on art and ethics (particularly Christian morals), her poems boldly remind their subjects and her readers again and again that it is an "Ethiop" (a Black) *who tells you* about these matters.

How remarkable that this enslaved young Black woman, barely an adolescent, dared speak with authority and earnest concern to male students at the most elite educational institution in the British colony of Massachusetts—bastion of the scions of colonial wealth and privilege, with much of that wealth founded on the trafficking of African peoples. That her world intersected theirs in such a fashion was another of the "difficult miracles" of Wheatley's life. Now, in 2023, 250 years after the publication of *Poems on Various Subjects, Religious and Moral*, Harvard University has installed a Black woman, Dr. Claudine Gay, at its helm as it also begins to seriously reckon with its deep complicity in the trans-Atlantic slave trade and slavery. Again, the "miracle"— the almost uncanny parallel of the enslaved and colonized young African negotiating the bounds of her status to subtly speak of race and increasingly of inequality in pre-Revolutionary America, and the precedent of a Black woman and leading scholar on the "relationship between race, gender, inequality, and political participation" determining the priorities of that educational center of power. Could Wheatley herself have imagined the possibility?

Imagine Phillis Wheatley Peters addressing Claudine Gay—without self-effacing preamble (no need!) to moderate her own agency and acts of provocation, or to mitigate the discomfiting topic of Harvard's entitlement and its sins… Imagine these Black women communing—across both the illusory divide of centuries and the broad stage of human history that connects them, each at the prompting of her liberatory consciousness… Imagine, too, the poet and the president both conversing with robust interest and in solidarity with today's students confronting the legacies of U.S. slavery and the challenges of intersectional systems of oppression, eschewing privilege in the quest for a new ethic of transformation.

To the University at Cambridge, in New-England,
a reinscription

for Phillis Wheatley Peters and Claudine Gay

I. Prologue
Call it history,
future, the web
of energies connecting
continents, diasporas...call it
synchronicity, fate spinning two lives,
spawning twined duties, twinned
by aboriginal homeplace, manifest genius...
such phenomena who compelled your colonized,
patriarchal halls to hear their voices.

If black and woman

    (Call them *miraculous, magical*...)

what has been required is
no less performance, no less

    (Call them *difficult*, their journeys...)

exceptional display
of the prodigious mind

    (Call them *timely, necessary*...)

of imagination
and the freedom

    (*Now?*)

to create anew.

II. Phillis
I tell you now, the public could not
know my thoughts fully—how much
their crimes perturbed me...
Why did Sturman Yenghis's bones
strung up in Peabody's vault,
and his skin tanned for a covering,
not arouse the outrage of Harvard's sons,

making them mutiny against that tyranny?
Why was, in truth, the entire archive of black and indigenous bodies
used up till spent (labor!) and used again (handy horror!)—
defiled, flayed, dissected, sprayed with bullets, broken, cuffed, choked
with license of this country's fears, constant across centuries—
the litany of such abuses—not enough to stir their conscience
even more than an abstract Jesus's salvation?
Today, my questions must be different, plainer…
Your concerns are not chiefly for piety,
or that good men alone must lead.
O, Harvard, are you enlightened yet?
And, how so? What holds you now in thrall,
with Christ ensconced in proper precinct
and men and women of every hue and rank
within your secular gates?

    III.

Of your new president, Dr. Claudine Gay,
black and a woman, of immigrant parents
from the first black nation in the Americas…
(If I had lived but twenty more years
to learn of Haiti's birth and honor
in verse its wresting of its sovereignty!)
I glean from this Sister's words her etiological
leaning: *We enter a moment of possibility. …*
We have a duty…to be of service to the world.
I endorse and echo her ethic of mutual care.
Students, what are your questions??
—by which I mean, what moves your minds and hearts?
Together, you'll shape the future by
the scope of your inquiry and ambition.
Make well-being a pursuit not for you alone,
but our common human and non-human home.
Another kind of slavery ensnares the "free"
who are blind to unjust causes and conditions.
I urge you, transcend the grasp of money

and privilege. Be more brave. More open.
Embrace compassion. Create justice.
In this you might seek redemption.

    IV.

A newer science tells of an invisible matter
comprising the main portion of
our galaxy...its unfathomable sway.
I knew as well the heft of what
is often overlooked. My will was
to show some of my own concerns,
although it mostly pleased the gentry
to witness a spectacle... And for a time
some sensed the intellect and heart in it.
I would sparkle with preternatural prowess!
But even as their patronage
eventually abandoned my family
to the hardship of poverty, I—
feeling always the quickening of my art—
would never forsake my own power
or the call to advocate and advise.
My spirit recognizes in our Sister Gay—
a comrade in letters—the same,
and for discerning it, too, I applaud you.

Although delivered from the dark abode
of a slaver's hold, I once happily had a life
that imbibed an African sun...a light
my soul did know and in the depths of
my consciousness reserved. I tell you,
it fueled me more than I could then profess.
Now, even more, though generations removed,
I would rouse in you a cosmic awareness—
unselfish...wholly relinquishing all
oppressions—better to preserve our
earthbound space, to traverse the ethereal

space, and mark the systems of revolution—
better for *all of us, moving forward together.*

To the University of Cambridge, in New-England

WHILE an intrinsic ardor prompts to write,
The muses promise to assist my pen;
'Twas not long since I left my native shore
The land of errors, and *Egyptian* gloom:
Father of mercy, 'twas thy gracious hand
Brought me in safety from those dark abodes.

   Students, to you 'tis giv'n to scan the heights
Above, to traverse the ethereal space,
And mark the systems of revolving worlds.
Still more, ye sons of science ye receive
The blissful news by messengers from heav'n,
How *Jesus'* blood for your redemption flows.
See him with hands out-stretcht upon the cross;
Immense compassion in his bosom glows;
He hears revilers, nor resents their scorn:
What matchless mercy in the Son of God!
When the whole human race by sin had fall'n,
He deign'd to die that they might rise again,
And share with him in the sublimest skies,
Life without death, and glory without end.

   Improve your privileges while they stay,
Ye pupils, and each hour redeem, that bears
Or good or bad report of you to heav'n.
Let sin, that baneful evil to the soul,
By you be shunn'd, nor once remit your guard;
Suppress the deadly serpent in its egg.
Ye blooming plants of human race divine,
An *Ethiop* tells you 'tis your greatest foe;
Its transient sweetness turns to endless pain,
And in immense perdition sinks the soul.

Artress Bethany White

Afric's Irony: A Word on Resistance

"To The Right Honorable William, Earl of Dartmouth, His Majesty's Principal Secretary of State for North America, &c." has always been one of my favorite poems to introduce to students when teaching Phillis Wheatley Peters, because it displays a skillful discursive pivot away from Revolutionary-era desire to Black liberation politics. Imagine the challenge of curbing a natural boldness, which Wheatley definitely embodied, in order to be seen as an appropriately civil Black girl while enmeshed in 18th-century Euro-American and European society. Wheatley was an adroit thinker, intellectual, and cosmopolitan of her day. Taking all aspects of her unique subject position into account, in my poem I capitalize on that essential pivot in Wheatley's original work in order to enhance the metonymic significance of the term Afric.

The diminutive of Africa was clearly an easier fit for the poet's use of iambic pentameter, but it also served to center the continent of Africa as a legitimate place where families, love, and culture abound. Wheatley fretted over her destiny, and what her life might have been if she had remained among her African countrymen. For Wheatley the page became a safe space to articulate, uncontested, the words of her heart. This form of Black resistance during enslavement often goes unremarked in American educational pedagogies daring to include the study of early African American literature. The page, unequivocally, provided a means for Wheatley to resist the racial status quo.

The term "African American," a nomenclature of descent, is meant to recall the rich history of the African continent and its global presence throughout the African diaspora. Today, so few in America are educated about the continent that the reference has become localized and deferential. Yet in Wheatley's era, the international slave trade was still in full operation, and Africa meant fresh human cargo easily translatable to saleable goods and wealth. I imagine a colonial-era Phillis caught up in the conundrum of why the masterminds behind the American Revolution could not make the leap from their fear of colonial white slavery to the need to simultaneously dismantle African enslavement with a single revolutionary act.

Tellingly, a mere two years after the publication of *Poems on Various Subjects, Religious and Moral*, Virginia governor Lord Dunmore would extend freedom to all indentured servants and "Negroes" who would cast off their rebel masters to fight for the British. In "To The Right Honorable William, Earl of Dartmouth, His Majesty's Principal Secretary of State for North America, &c." Wheatley is aware of how the status of Blacks in the colonies is ripe for change, and that change is in the hands of the British-American peerage reigning over them. In using the term Afric' in her poem, the African American poet is demanding to be seen by recalling the continent that produced her and her fellow Africans still being wrongfully monetized for global greed.

To the Right Honourable William, Earl of Dartmouth, His Majesty's Principal Secretary of State for North America, &c.,
a reinscription

Imagine, freedom embraces a new day
ending threats of war on tense New England shores
all thanks to Dartmouth changing the course
of history, and bending the King's ear to help
him see, that America is indeed free
and not a new land for white and Black slavery.

Imagine, I know all about slavery.
Recall the loose-limbed strut of the once free
before being torn with a *Please, help!*
from parents at dawn and set on a ship's course
whisking this Black girl far from *Afric's* shores
to pen poems for freedom from Britain day.

Is it resentment you think you hear so free
in my verse brimming with coupled pleas to help
you remember me? *Afric*, short of course
for Black sorrow on American shores,
the endless wait for emancipation day
to firmly cast off manacled slavery.

Great men crave fame, but few extend help
to humans in pain. Freedom their right, of course,
but we all covet liberty on near and far shores.
Even you, Dartmouth, will stand one day
beneath God's sternest glare—hopeful and free
or bedeviled for endorsing slavery.

To the Right Honourable William, Earl of Dartmouth, His Majesty's Principal Secretary of State for North America, &c.

HAIL, happy day, when, smiling like the morn,
Fair *Freedom* rose *New-England* to adorn:
The northern clime beneath her genial ray,
Dartmouth, congratulates thy blissful sway:
Elate with hope her race no longer mourns,
Each soul expands, each grateful bosom burns,
While in thine hand with pleasure we behold
The silken reins, and *Freedom's* charms unfold.
Long lost to realms beneath the northern skies
She shines supreme, while hated *faction* dies:
Soon as appear'd the *Goddess* long desir'd,
Sick at the view, she languish'd and expir'd;
Thus from the splendors of the morning light
The owl in sadness seeks the caves of night

No more, *America*, in mournful strain
Of wrongs, and grievance unredress'd complain,
No longer shalt thou dread the iron chain,
Which wanton *Tyranny* with lawless hand
Had made, and with it meant t'enslave the land.

Should you, my lord, while you peruse my song,
Wonder from whence my love of *Freedom* sprung,
Whence flow these wishes for the common good,
By feeling hearts alone best understood,
I, young in life, by seeming cruel fate
Was snatch'd from *Afric's* fancy'd happy seat:
What pangs excruciating must molest,
What sorrows labour in my parent's breast?
Steel'd was that soul and by no misery mov'd
That from a father seiz'd his babe belov'd:

Such, such my case. And can I then but pray
Others may never feel tyrannic sway?

For favours past, great Sir, our thanks are due,
And thee we ask thy favours to renew,
Since in thy pow'r, as in thy will before,
To sooth the griefs, which thou did'st once deplore.
May heav'nly grace the sacred sanction give
To all thy works, and thou for ever live
Not only on the wings of fleeting *Fame*,
Though praise immortal crowns the patriot's name,
But to conduct to heav'ns refulgent fane,
May fiery coursers sweep th'ethereal plain,
And bear thee upwards to that blest abode,
Where, like the prophet, thou shalt find thy God.

Evie Shockley

Phillis Wheatley Peters was Able to Thank "S.P.G." Using the "Art" He May Have Helped Her to Develop

I initially conceived of the editors' invitation as the challenge of trying to imagine how Phillis Wheatley Peters might approach her poem's subject if she were a young woman writing today. But what *was* the subject of "An Hymn to Humanity," really? I hadn't taught or studied this poem, admittedly in part because I couldn't determine what was motivating her to celebrate "humanity." Who was the "S.P.G." to whom the poem was dedicated? There was no information about this mystery in the Schomburg edition of Wheatley's poems I'd always worked with. My search for scholarship that might answer the question led to no reading of the poem that cohered productively or satisfied my curiosity. Finally, a finding aid for the Wheatley archives at Emory University led me to the online facsimile of an 18th-century copybook containing a variant version of her poem, in which the dedication read "To S.P. Gallowy Esq: who corrected some Poetic Essays of the Authoress." Once I understood that Wheatley's poem was inspired by gratitude toward a person who had helped her—the self-described "languid muse in low degree"—learn her craft, I knew what I would write. My poem could speak to/through Wheatley's by expressing gratitude to someone who had supported my desire to pursue poetry when I was a young Black writer in a very white environment that was often discouraging and at times felt actively hostile. (Afric's muse does not forgetful prove, whether in the 18th or 21st century.) In terms of poetics, I tried to echo Wheatley's conceptual and formal structure: opening, as she does, with a wide-lens view of humankind before zooming in on two particular figures; and giving my stanzas a shape and pattern similar to hers, but with a different, less regular-sounding meter. Wheatley was able to thank "S.P.G." using the "Art" he may have helped her to develop. I'm glad to be able to make my own thank-you to "A.S." in the same fashion.

HUMANITY
—for a.s.

of all the ways the atoms
    can align, they form adams
sometimes: of & on the earth.
    some such see themselves as gods.
some see that uneven odds
    distort how we measure worth.

the universe sometimes takes
    care of its creatures, but breaks
us just as often. we can't
    rule the planets, but can try
to bring *ourselves* to supply
    each other the care we each want.

yo: a young black poet longs,
    like her guide, to write, right wrongs.
he mentors her, urges her
    through a door racism would
have held closed (but that *he* could
    open), encourages her.

he sees in her a quiet
    fire. she doesn't deny it ::
but his eye seems to quicken
    its slow burn. though we won't call
this *virtue*, we approve all
    human gestures that thicken

justice. when time comes that he
    leaves, her love of poetry
stays lit: words, lines still thronging.
    & she remembers, later—
when she's read by a hater
    who questions her belonging—

this man, who didn't have to,
　　befriended her work :: he knew
(didn't *know*, but hoped) her muse
　　would rise, shine, & sing someday,
finding her brown-colored clay
　　a divine channel to choose.

An Hymn to Humanity
To S. P. G. Esq;

I.

LO! for this dark terrestrial ball
Forsakes his azure-paved hall
    A prince of heav'nly birth!
Divine *Humanity* behold,
What wonders rise, what charms unfold
    At his descent to earth!

II.

The bosoms of the great and good
With wonder and delight he view'd,
    And fix'd his empire there:
Him, close compressing to his breast,
The sire of gods and men address'd,
    "My son, my heav'nly fair!

III.

"Descend to earth, there place thy throne;
"To succour man's afflicted son
    "Each human heart inspire:
"To act in bounties unconfin'd
"Enlarge the close contracted mind,
    "And fill it with thy fire."

IV.

Quick as the word, with swift career
He wings his course from star to star,
    And leaves the bright abode.
The *Virtue* did his charms impart;
Their G___! then thy raptur'd heart
    Perceiv'd the rushing God:

V.

For when thy pitying eye did see
The languid muse in low degree,
    Then, then at thy desire
Descended the celestial nine;
O'er me methought they deign'd to shine,
    And deign'd to string my lyre.

VI.

Can *Afric's* muse forgetful prove?
Or can such friendship fail to move
    A tender human heart?
Immortal *Friendship* laurel-crown'd
The smiling *Graces* all surround
    With ev'ry heav'nly *Art.*

Contributors

TARA BETTS is the author of *Refuse to Disappear*, *Break the Habit*, and *Arc & Hue*. She teaches at DePaul University and serves as poetry editor of *The Langston Hughes Review*.

LILLIAN-YVONNE BERTRAM is the author of *Travesty Generator* (Noemi Press), a book of computational poetry that received the Poetry Society of America's 2020 Anna Rabinowitz prize for interdisciplinary work and was longlisted for the 2020 National Book Award for Poetry. They are the recipient of a National Endowment for the Arts Poetry Fellowship. Their other poetry books include *How Narrow My Escapes* (DIAGRAM/New Michigan Press), *Personal Science* (Tupelo Press), *a slice from the cake made of air* (Red Hen Press), and *But a Storm is Blowing From Paradise* (Red Hen Press). Their fifth book, *Negative Money* (Soft Skull Press), is available now.

MAHOGANY L. BROWNE is executive director of JustMedia; artistic director of Urban Word; and a writer, playwright, and organizer. She has received fellowships from the Kennedy Center, Cave Canem, the Mellon Foundation, and the Rauschenberg Foundation. The author of YA novels, children's books, anthologies, plays, and poetry collections, Browne is the first ever poet-in-residence at Lincoln Center and lives in Brooklyn.

GABRIELLE CIVIL is a black feminist performance artist, poet, and writer originally from Detroit, Michigan. She has premiered more than 50 performance artworks worldwide, including *Translated Bodies* (2023), *the déjà vu — live* (2022), and *Jupiter* (2021). Her performance memoirs include *Swallow the Fish* (2017), *Experiments in Joy* (2019), *(ghost gestures)* (2021), and *the déjà vu* (2022). Her writing has also appeared in *New Daughters of Africa*, *Kitchen Table Translation*, *Migrating Pedagogies*, and *Experiments in Joy: A Workbook*. A 2023 Franconia Performance Fellow, she teaches at the California Institute of the Arts. The aim of her work is to open up space.

L'MERCHIE FRAZIER is a Boston-based visual artist, educator, poet, and consultant. She is executive director of Creative and Strategic Partnerships of SPOKE Art, and serves as an art commissioner for the Commonwealth of Massachusetts. A 25-year member of the Women of Color Quilter's Network, she has been praised for her evocative fiber and metal sculptures, innovative mixed media installations, and powerful quilt series the "Quilted Chronicles." Her work has been exhibited in the public and private collections of institutions including the University of Vermont, the American Museum of Art and Design, the White House, and the Smithsonian Institution and appeared in publications including *A History of Art in Africa*, *International Review of African American Art*, *Journey of Hope: Quilts Inspired by President Barack Obama*, and *Spirits of the Cloth*.

DANIELLE LEGROS GEORGES is a poet, translator, and editor who works in the areas of contemporary U.S. poetry, Black and African-diasporic poetry and literature, and Caribbean/Latin American and Haitian studies. Her work has been supported by fellowships and grants from institutions including the American Antiquarian Society, the Boston Foundation, the Massachusetts Cultural Council, the PEN/Heim Translation Fund, and the Black Metropolis Research Consortium. In 2014 she was named poet laureate of the city of Boston. Her four-year term included collaborations with area artists, literary organizations, museums, libraries, and schools; and representation of Boston at international events. She is professor emeritus of creative writing at Lesley University.

ARACELIS GIRMAY is a poet, teacher, and editor and makes works across genres. She is the author of three collections of poems, most recently *the black maria* (BOA Editions, 2016). For her work she was a finalist for the Neustadt International Prize for Literature. girmay is on the editorial board of the African Poetry Book Fund and is the current editor-at-large of the Blessing the Boats Selections.

TSITSI JAJI is the author of *Mother Tongues* (2019 Cave Canem Northwestern University Press Prize); *Beating the Graves* (2017); a chapbook, *Carnaval* (2014) from African Poetry Book Fund; and a book of research: *Africa in Stereo: Music, Modernism and Pan-African Solidarity.* Jaji was born and raised in Zimbabwe. Her poems, which often evoke music, the sacred, migrancy, and ecological crisis, have appeared in *Transition, The Atlantic, The Harvard Review,* and *Poem-a-Day* and in several musical works.

YALIE SAWEDA KAMARA is a Sierra Leonean American writer, educator, and researcher from Oakland, California. She is the 2022-2023 Cincinnati and Mercantile Library Poet Laureate (two-year term) and the winner of the 2023 Elizabeth Alexander Award for Poetry and the 2022-2023 Jake Adam York Prize. Her forthcoming debut poetry collection, *Besaydoo*, will be published by Milkweed Editions in 2024. Kamara earned a Ph.D. in creative writing and English literature from the University of Cincinnati. She resides in Cincinnati, where she is assistant professor of English at Xavier University. For more information visit her website: www.yaylala.com

DONIKA KELLY is the author of *The Renunciations* and *Bestiary.* A recipient of a fellowship from the National Endowment for the Arts, she is a Cave Canem graduate fellow and founding member of the collective Poets at the End of the World. She currently lives in Iowa City, Iowa, where she teaches creative writing at the University of Iowa.

ROSAMOND S. KING, a TrinbaGambian writer and performer, often draws on reality to create nonliteral culturally and politically engaged interpretations of African and diaspora experiences. King is the author of the poetry collections *All the Rage* (Nightboat Books) and the Lambda Award-winning *Rock / Salt / Stone* (Nightboat Books). Her monograph *Island Bodies: Transgressive Sexualities in the Carib-bean Imagination* won the Caribbean Studies Association best book award. King's writing has also been published in more than three dozen journals, blogs, and anthologies, and she has performed at biennales, festivals, and other venues around the world. For more information visit her website: www.rosamondSking.black.com

FLORENCE LADD has had an extensive academic career and also published two novels, *Sarah's Psalm* and *The Spirit of Josephine*. She has issued two chapbooks: *Reclaiming Rose: A Suite of Poems* and *Le Chevalier de Saint-Georges and His Mother: An Epic*. Other poems have been published in *The Women's Review of Books*, *The Progressive*, *The Rockhurst Review*, *Sweet Auburn*, *Beyond Slavery*, *Transition*, *The Golden Shovel Anthology*, *MUSE*, *Oberon*, and *Renga for Obama*. A collection of her poems is in progress. She co-founded Langston's Legacy, a collective of poets. She lived in Cambridge, Massachusetts, for decades, and now lives in a village in France.

JANICE A. LOWE is a composer-poet and multi-instrumentalist. Her work has been recognized by Creative Capital, MacDowell, City Artists Corps, The Rauschenberg Foundation, and The Center for Contemporary Writing at the University of Pennsylvania. Lowe has performed/recorded with bands including w/o a net; Julie Ezelle Patton's Rock, Paper, Sisters; Anne Waldman & Fast Speaking Music; and Irreversible Entanglements. Her musical theater compositions include *Lil Budda*, text by Stephanie L. Jones. She was commissioned to compose musical settings of poems from the Pulitzer Prize–awarded collection *Olio* by poet Tyehimba Jess. Lowe holds an MFA in musical theater composition from New York University. She is a co-founder of the Dark Room Collective. For more information visit her website: www.janicelowe.com

SHARA MCCALLUM has published six books in the United States and the United Kingdom, including her most recent, *No Ruined Stone*, winner of the 2022 Hurston/Wright Legacy Award for Poetry. An anthology of her poems translated into Spanish by Adalber Salas Hernández, *La historia es un cuarto*, was published in 2021 in Mexico. McCallum is Edwin Erle Sparks Professor of English at Penn State University, is on the faculty of the Pacific University Low-residency MFA, and served as the 2021-22 Penn State Laureate. She is a 2023 Guggenheim Fellow. For more information visit her website: www.sharamccallum.com

PAMELA MORDECAI was born in Jamaica. A former language arts teacher with a Ph.D. in English, she was for 14 years editor of the *Caribbean Journal of Education*. She is the author of more than 30 books, including textbooks, children's books, anthologies, nine collections of poetry, a reference work on Jamaica, a collection of short fiction, and a novel. She has edited ground-breaking anthologies of Caribbean women's writing. In 2010 her play *El Numero Uno* premiered at the Loraine Kimsa Theatre for Young People and in March 2016 had its Caribbean premiere at the Edna Manley School for the Performing and Visual Arts. Her debut novel *Red Jacket* was one of five books shortlisted for the Rogers Writers' Trust Fiction Award in 2015.

KIKI PETROSINO is the author of *White Blood: A Lyric of Virginia* (2020) and three other poetry books, all from Sarabande Books. She holds graduate degrees from the University of Chicago and the University of Iowa Writer's Workshop. Her memoir, *Bright*, was released from Sarabande in 2022. She directs the creative writing program at the University of Virginia, where she is professor of poetry. Petrosino is the recipient of a MacDowell artist residency, a Pushcart Prize, a Fellowship in Creative Writing from the National Endowment for the Arts, the UNT Rilke Prize, and the Spalding Prize, among other honors.

EVIE SHOCKLEY thinks, creates, and writes with her eye on a Black feminist horizon. Her books of poetry include *suddenly we*, *semiautomatic*, and *the new black*. Her work has garnered the Hurston/ Wright Legacy Award, made her a finalist for the Pulitzer Prize, and appeared internationally. Her honors include the Poetry Society of America's Shelley Memorial Award, the Lannan Literary Award for Poetry, the Holmes National Poetry Prize, and the Stephen Henderson Award. Her joys include participating in poetry communities such as Cave Canem and collaborating with like-minded artists. Shockley is the Zora Neale Hurston Distinguished Professor of English at Rutgers University.

TRACY K. SMITH is a librettist, translator, and author of five acclaimed poetry collections. From 2017 to 2019, she served as the 22d Poet Laureate of the United States. A professor of English and of African and African American Studies at Harvard University, her most recent book is *To Free the Captives: A Plea for the American Soul.*

SHARAN STRANGE's recent writings are in *The Art Section: An Online Journal of Art and Cultural Commentary*; *Aunt Chloe: A Journal of Artful Candor*; *Furious Flower: Seeding the Future of African American Poetry*; and, *Bigger Than Bravery: Black Resilience and Reclamation in a Time of Pandemic.* She has also created works for gallery and museum exhibitions in New York, Boston, Atlanta, Oakland, and Seattle, and her collaborations with composers have been performed by American Modern Ensemble, The Dream Unfinished Orchestra, and International Contemporary Ensemble, among others. She is currently at work on a libretto for an opera slated for production in 2024.

ARTRESS BETHANY WHITE, associate professor of English at East Stroudsburg University, is a poet, essayist, and literary critic. She is the recipient of the Trio Award for her poetry collection *My Afmerica: poems* (Trio House Press, 2019). Her prose, *Survivor's Guilt: Essays on Race and American Identity*, received a 2022 Next Generation Finalist Indie Book Award. Recent work appears in the anthology *Why I Wrote This Poem: 62 Poets on Creativity and Craft.* White has received scholarships and residencies from the Sewanee Writers' Conference and Bread Loaf. For more information visit her website: artressbethanywhite.com

www.ingramcontent.com/pod-product-compliance
Lightning Source LLC
Chambersburg PA
CBHW020403130626
46549CB00006B/2413